Realizing Happiness
A Perceptive Study of Biblical Happiness

Realizing Happiness

A Perceptive Study of Biblical Happiness

Marcus E. Turner. Sr.

Copyright © 2012 by Marcus E. Turner, Sr.

All rights reserved. Written permission must be secured from publisher to use or reproduce any part of this book except for brief quotations in critical reviews or articles.

Scripture quotations without marking are taken from the King James Version. The King James Version is in the public domain except in the United Kingdom; no permission necessary for use of Scripture.

Scripture quotations marked "BBE" are taken from the Bible in Basic English. The Bible in Basic English is in the public domain; no permission necessary for use of Scripture.

Scripture quotations marked "GW" are taken from GOD'S WORD. GOD'S WORD is a copyrighted work of God's Word to the Nations. Quotations are used by permission. Copyright © 1995 by God's Word to the Nations. All rights reserved.

Scripture quotations marked "NKJV" are taken from the New King James Version®. Copyright © 1982 by Thomas Nelson, Inc. Used by permission. All rights reserved.

Scripture taken from the Amplified Bible, Copyright © 1954, 1958, 1962, 1964, 1965, 1987 by The Lockman Foundation. Used by permission.

Scripture quotations marked (NIV) are taken from the HOLY BIBLE, NEW INTERNATIONAL VERSION®. NIV®. Copyright© 1973, 1978, 1984 by International Bible Society. Used by permission of Zondervan. All rights reserved.

Scripture quotations from THE MESSAGE. Copyright © by Eugene H. Peterson 1993, 1994, 1995, 1996, 2000, 2001, 2002. Used by permission of NavPress Publishing Group.

Realizing Happiness: A Perceptive Study of Biblical Happiness

International Standard Book Number—10:0-9799414-0-7
International Standard Book Number—13:978-0-9799414-0-5
Library of Congress Control Number—2007937791

Printed in the United States of America

This book is dedicated to my beloved wife, Lisa, my four wonderful children, Marcus, Gabrielle, Victoria, and Bethany, and my Christian parents, Robert L. and Hazel L. Turner.

Contents

Introduction	9
Longing for Happiness	11
Truths You Should Know	21
The Biblical Meaning of the Word "Happy"	35
God Wants You to Be Happy	45
Happiness Can Be Yours	57
Happiness Can Be Yours—Part 2	73
Your Character is Important	89
The Happy Experience	105
Faith Declarations	119
About the Author	129

Introduction

In 2007 I was inspired to teach a series of messages to my congregation that centered on happiness. The title of the series was "Blessed." I used that particular title because it seemed most fitting. The word "blessed" is a very familiar cliché used regularly by people of all walks of life, and especially by Christians. Even nonbelievers have grown accustomed to thinking about how grateful they are for their lives and how appreciative they are of all the good things life has given them. Usually the phrase used to convey these thoughts of nonbelievers is "I'm blessed." In Christendom the phrase is very popular. It can be heard from the mouths of pastors, ministers, deacons, psalmists, radio hosts, television personalities, etc. The word has almost become iconic. I can say with confidence that it is nearly impossible to be in what is considered a Christian venue and not hear someone say "I'm blessed" or "blessed and highly favored."

In general the word connotes I'm fine, I'm favored, I'm cool, what has happened or is happening is not by chance but on purpose, things are going right in my life. Its vocabulary has widened over time because of the vast usage of the word. In my opinion, the word has weakened through the years. During the late twelfth century, the word "blessed" implied "supremely happy" thus inferring the phrase I'm blessed to mean I'm supremely happy. This implication is much closer to what I feel the biblical implication of the word means. It, like many other terms, has suffered etymological erosion from the continual water drip of time.

As you will learn in the pages to come, the word "blessed" in the Bible, more than anything else, aligns itself with the word "happy." Therefore, to hear someone say they are blessed fundamentally means they are supremely happy: "I'm blessed—I'm supremely happy. You are blessed—you are supremely happy. Blessed are the...—Supremely happy are the..."

My goal for this book is to examine the primary Old and New Testament scriptures on happiness and point out the biblical evidence that supports biblical happiness. This book follows a study guide format to enhance your spiritual awareness and growth. Regardless of your plight, condition, or situation, you have a biblical right to be blessed, to be supremely happy. After reading this book, I pray you will be able to say with confidence and assurance "I'm blessed—I'm supremely happy."

Marcus E. Turner, Sr.

Chapter 1

Longing for Happiness

Oh that men would praise the LORD for his goodness, and for his wonderful works to the children of men! For he satisfieth the longing soul, and filleth the hungry soul with goodness.
Psalms 107:8–9

It has been said that only a small percentage of Americans are happy. Fewer Americans are happy today than they were thirty years ago, thanks to longer working hours, greed, lack of purpose, war, the present-day recession, and deterioration in the quality of their relationships with family, friends, and neighbors. If this is true, you can understand the urgency behind my writing this book. Americans are looking and searching, longing for happiness. Therefore, it goes without saying, Christians also make up a large percentage of unhappy Americans. This fact is the fuel powering my motivation to write to Christians and inform them that they do not belong in that percentage of unhappy people. It is not the will of God for Christians to live in an unhappy state.

> John 16:33—*These things I have spoken unto you, that in me ye might have peace. In the world ye shall have tribulation: but be of good cheer; I have overcome the world.*

God has a plan for your happiness. God wants you to be happy. But as long as you are pursuing happiness according to the world's standards and means, you will never achieve happiness. Conversely, if for some reason you do, it will never sustain the test of time. You must discover God's ordained plan of happiness.

> Psalm 37:23 (MSG)—*Stalwart walks in step with God; his path blazed by God, he's happy.*

What is biblical happiness? What does God have to say about your happiness? Does God want you to be happy? Is there something you can do to sustain your happiness? These questions are answered in this book, and I hope you will find that you are closer to attaining happiness in your life than you realized.

The following two assumptions serve as the foundation of this book:

> 1. The Bible in its entirety is the unadulterated Word of God. Therefore, what the Bible says on a subject is God's view of that subject.

> 2. Biblical happiness will never be achieved outside of salvation. The first step toward your happiness is to accept God's way of deliverance.

One of the greatest acts of kindness performed in the history of mankind was when God the Father in His infinite love released His Son, Jesus, to us—giving us another opportunity to regain what we lost in the Garden of Eden: eternal life and fellowship with God.

> John 3:16 (NKJV)—*For God so loved the world that He gave His only begotten Son, that whoever believes in Him should not perish but have everlasting life.*

It is my belief that the only way to recoup eternal life and fellowship with God is through Jesus the Christ.

> John 14:6—*Jesus saith unto him, I am the way, the truth, and the life: No man cometh unto the Father, but by me.*

In addition I believe salvation takes place when a sinner

recognizes his sinful and hopeless state, hears the unadulterated Word of God that demands repentance of sins, and then confesses with his mouth and believes in his heart the saving grace of God. My belief is strengthened by the apostle Paul's words, in the Book of Romans, chapter ten.

> Romans 10:9 (NKJV)—*That if you confess with your mouth the Lord Jesus and believe in your heart that God has raised Him from the dead, you will be saved.*

> John 20:29 (AMP)—*Jesus said to him, Because you have seen Me, Thomas, do you now believe (trust, have faith)? Blessed and happy and to be envied are those who have never seen Me and yet have believed and adhered to and trusted and relied on Me.*

This book is written out of my own personal journey for happiness. It is an amazing thing to grow up in a society that constantly floods your mind with ideas and images of happiness, only to discover that this world is incapable of providing eternal happiness. My journey was full of frustration and disappointments; I was frustrated with my life and disappointed with myself, my status, and my predicament. All my efforts were useless or, in the word of Solomon, vanity.

> Ecclesiastes 1:14 (AMP)—*I have seen all the works that are done under the sun, and behold, all is vanity, a striving after the wind and a feeding on wind.*

The apostle John gave a stern warning about seeking the happiness of the world.

> 1 John 2:15–17 (NKJV)—*Do not love the world or the things in the world. If anyone loves the world, the love of the Father is not in him. For all that is in the world—the lust of the flesh, the lust of the eyes, and the pride of life—is not of the Father but is of the world. And the world*

is passing away, and the lust of it; but he who does the will of God abides forever.

My breakthrough in life came once I discovered that the Lord needed to constantly be the builder of my life. It is easy to allow God to build the walls of your life in the area of salvation and then fire Him as the builder of the remaining years of your life. Many Christians are content with the initial salvation experience. But it is the sanctification process that shapes us into the Lord's image. It is during this time God molds us into the persons He desires us to be, prepares us for the tasks we must do, and allows us to live life abundantly—and happily.

David expressed his thoughts concerning life lived without the Lord.

Psalm 127:1 (NKJV)—*Unless the Lord builds the house, They labor in vain who build it; Unless the Lord guards the city, The watchman stays awake in vain.*

David declared life is useless without God. Your efforts will be hopeless unless God intervenes. I believe God in His infinite wisdom sent His Son, Jesus, to rescue us from our hopelessness and futile efforts.

Matthew 11:28 (NKJV)—*Come to Me, all you who labor and are heavy laden, and I will give you rest.*

When I truly began searching the Bible, walking by faith and not by sight, and allowing God to be the reigning King in my life (LORD), I discovered God's plan for happiness. Now I want to share this deliverance opportunity with you. Regardless of your plight, condition, or situation, you can be happy. God wants you to be happy. So you *can* be as happy as you want to be.

When Moses died Joshua assumed leadership over the children of Israel. Joshua was new, nervous, and naïve but chosen.

Longing for Happiness

God made a profound promise to Joshua.

> Joshua 1:8 (AMP)—*This Book of the Law shall not depart out of your mouth, but you shall meditate on it day and night, that you may observe and do according to all that is written in it. For then you shall make your way prosperous, and then you shall deal wisely and have good success.*

God promised Joshua a prosperous journey and good success, a state of happiness, if he would be faithful to learn and obey His Word. I believe God has promised Christians the same state of happiness if we would be faithful to learn and obey His Word. The Bible is thorough in its discussion on biblical happiness. Grab your Bible, notepad, and pen, and join me in discovering biblical happiness.

Questions to Ask and Answer

1. With the percentage of happy Americans being so low, how important is it to discover God's view on happiness?

2. Is it the will of God for believers to live in happiness? (Read Psalm 1:1.)

3. Does God have an established plan for your happiness? (Read Jeremiah 29:11.)

4. Is God's plan linked to the world's source of happiness? (Read 1 John 2:15; James 4:4.)

5. Do you agree with the two assumptions found in this chapter? Have you experienced salvation?

6. After salvation what things usually must occur to discover God's plan for happiness?

Chapter 1

Longing for Happiness

Memory Verse: Psalm 107:8–9—*Oh that men would praise the LORD for his goodness, and for his wonderful works to the children of men! For he satisfieth the longing soul, and filleth the hungry soul with goodness.*

1. Read Psalm 107:8–9 aloud. What do these verses teach about God's wonderful works for the longing and hungry soul?

_____

_____

2. Read John 16:33 aloud. What does this verse teach about God's willingness to share wisdom to His disciples so they might have peace?

_____

_____

Longing for Happiness

What reason does God gives His disciples to keep cheerful, even in a world of tribulations?

_____

_____

How does this reason relate to you as a Christian? (Read 1 John 5:4–5; Romans 6:4.)

_____

_____

3. Many people on their personal pursuit of happiness encounter frustration. Read Psalm 127:1 aloud. Why do you believe it is true?

_____

_____

4. Read Joshua 1:8 aloud. What were the prerequisites given to Joshua, by God, before he could experience prosperity and good success?

_____

_____

5. "Stalwart walks in step with GOD; his path blazed by GOD, he's happy" (Ps. 37:23 MSG). Take a few moments to reflect on this verse. Compare it with other Bible translations.

_____

_____

6. Reflect on the two assumptions given as the foundation of this study. What are your thoughts and comments (Do you agree with them? Are you willing to accept God's judgment on a subject, even if it is contrary to your existing belief? What is God's way of deliverance? Are you saved?)?

_____
_____
_____
_____
_____
_____
_____
_____
_____
_____
_____
_____
_____
_____

Chapter 2

Truths You Should Know

And you will have knowledge of what is true, and that will make you free.
John 8:32 (BBE)

There are four truths you need to grasp before moving forward. These truths about happiness will help you dispel the myths you have heard and stand on the truth you know.

The world will not always understand

Your status before God will not always be expressed in a manner modern-day society considers as being happy. For example, you receive news that your loved one was in a car accident. According to the police officers and tow-truck drivers, the car was totaled. Yet your loved one was not badly injured. It is a blessing just to think he or she survived. Now, as you conclude your telephone call, you begin rejoicing in the Lord for His goodness and His favor. But a coworker overheard your telephone call, and now he is observing the strange way you are acting in the midst of misfortune.

"Why are you, of all people, so happy?" he shouts.

"Because my loved one is safe and unharmed," you reply.

"But you just bought that car six months ago…you should be furious right now. I know I would be."

The world will not understand your happiness.

Such is the case with David when his son died. The elders of his family were concerned with his desperate response when his son was sick; however, they were more concerned with his apparent happiness when his son died.

After Nathan went home, God afflicted the child that Uriah's wife bore to David, and the child became sick. David prayed desperately to God for the little boy. He fasted, wouldn't go out, and slept on the floor. The elders in his family came in and tried to get him off the floor, but he wouldn't budge. Nor could they get him to eat anything. On the seventh day, the child died. David's servants were afraid to tell him. They said, "What do we do now? While the child was living he wouldn't listen to a word we said. Now, with the child dead, if we speak to him there's no telling what he'll do." David got up from the floor, washed his face and combed his hair, put on a fresh change of clothes, then went into the sanctuary and worshiped. Then he came home and asked for something to eat. They set it before him, and he ate. His servants asked him, "What's going on with you?" (2 Sam. 12:15–21 MSG.)

The concept of happiness is spiritual. It is beyond worldly comprehension. Be very careful in your understanding of biblical happiness and its comparison to worldly happiness. You will always open the door to disappointment and despair whenever you leave God's view of happiness to follow man's view. Be very careful who you listen to for the daily forecast of your life.

Happiness may not always be perceptible

The state of happiness God wants you to enjoy may not always seem to be happy. Happiness is not based upon visual appearances, audible words, or emotional hunches. It is based upon a strong belief system in the Almighty. You will never achieve happiness by living life solely in the physical realm. You must tap into the spiritual realm.

Jesus put an end to the "physical realm only" theory.

John 4:24 (NKJV)—*God is Spirit, and those who worship Him must worship in spirit and truth.*

John 17:16 (AMP)—*They are not of the world (worldly, belonging to the world), [just] as I am not of the world.*

Paul sustained the argument by insisting that Christians live life beyond this world.

2 Corinthians 4:18 (NKJV)—*While we do not look at the things which are seen, but at the things which are not seen. For the things which are seen are temporary, but the things which are not seen are eternal.*

The world is too perverted and dim to rely upon visual appearances, audible words, or emotional hunches. If you desire happiness—the God-intended happiness—you must see life through the eyes of faith.

Hebrews 11:1&6 (NIV)—*Now faith is being sure of what we hope for and certain of what we do not see...And without faith it is impossible to please God, because anyone who comes to him must believe that he exists and that he rewards those who earnestly seek him.*

Romans 1:17—*For therein is the righteousness of God revealed from faith to faith: as it is written, The just shall live by faith.*

2 Cor 5:7 (NIV)—*We live by faith, not by sight.*

In Romans 4 Paul told the story of Abraham's faith. God appeared to Abraham and declared that Abraham and his wife, Sarah, would have a son. Now Abraham was well into his nineties, and Sarah was barren. Abraham, however, maintained a state of hope, praise, and satisfaction (happiness) in the midst of a situation that seemed hopeless.

Paul attributed Abraham's ability to remain happy to his willingness to operate in the spiritual realm by trusting God.

> Romans 4:18—*Who against hope believed in hope, that he might become the father of many nations, according to that which was spoken, So shall thy seed be.*

Though it resembles the world's happiness… it is not

The world will perceive you as happy based on its standards—money, wealth, promotion, and accomplishments (things you will acquire and lose)—but your happiness will be rooted in Christianity. You have to make up your mind early: "I am what I am because of the unmerited favor of Almighty God." If not, pride will creep in unnoticed and ruin your happiness. Beware in your happiness. Do not forget "the bridge that brought you over"—the grace of God.

One of the greatest passages of Scripture that teaches this particular principle is Deuteronomy 8:11–20 (NKJV):

> *Beware that you do not forget the Lord your God by not keeping His commandments, His judgments, and His statutes which I command you today, lest--when you have eaten and are full, and have built beautiful houses and dwell in them; and when your herds and your flocks multiply, and your silver and your gold are multiplied, and all that you have is multiplied; when your heart is lifted up, and you forget the Lord your God who brought you out of the land of Egypt, from the house of bondage; who led you through that great and terrible wilderness, in which were fiery serpents and scorpions and thirsty land where there was no water; who brought water for you out of the flinty rock; who fed you in the wilderness with manna,*

which your fathers did not know, that He might humble you and that He might test you, to do you good in the end--then you say in your heart, 'My power and the might of my hand have gained me this wealth.' And you shall remember the Lord your God, for it is He who gives you power to get wealth, that He may establish His covenant which He swore to your fathers, as it is this day. Then it shall be, if you by any means forget the Lord your God, and follow other gods, and serve them and worship them, I testify against you this day that you shall surely perish. As the nations which the Lord destroys before you, so you shall perish, because you would not be obedient to the voice of the Lord your God.

Moses in his wisdom and understanding cried out to the children of Israel: *It was God; it is God; it will be God!* It is important you realize regardless of how blessed you are and how happy you become, it is God. As God blesses you, the world will congratulate you for your success. It will name the contributing factors to your success and will ask you to boast. Beware! You must remain levelheaded, and give God all the credit.

Acts 17:28 (MSG)—*We live and move in him, can't get away from him! One of your poets said it well: 'We're the God-created.*

Look at Paul's great testimony on his happy state:

Philippians 4:10–13 (MSG)—*I'm glad in God, far happier than you would ever guess - happy that you're again showing such strong concern for me. Not that you ever quit praying and thinking about me. You just had no chance to show it. Actually, I don't have a sense of needing anything personally. I've learned by now to be quite content whatever my circumstances. I'm just as happy with little as with much, with much as with little. I've found the recipe for being happy whether full or hungry, hands full or hands empty. Whatever I have, wherever I am, I can make it through anything in the One who makes me who I am.*

Regardless of where he momentarily found himself in the world's perception of happiness, Paul stated that he was able to maintain his contentment with life (happiness) without becoming prideful because his foundation for happiness was not built on the world's perception. It was built on his relationship with God through Jesus Christ. It is my prayer that God will "enlarge your territory" and prosper you tenfold. Nonetheless, it is also my prayer that you will remain focused *on* Him and His agenda.

Happiness begets success

The second most desired thing after happiness is success. Modern society is full of individuals fighting to acquire it. The longings for happiness and success are so ongoing they begin to blend and become disproportionate. You start hearing things like, "If I could find success, then I would find happiness," and "If only I could land a successful job or, better yet, find the right person, then I would be happy." That type of thinking may sound logical to some, but it is not biblical.

It is from walking in biblical happiness, the blessed state of being in God's will, that you will be able to successfully face life in every arena. The world's happiness will never satisfy the inner voids of our lives; only the Lord can satisfy our emptiness. Then, once satisfied, you can freely and wisely progress through life under the direction of the Holy Spirit.

Proverbs 3:1–4 (NKJV)—My son, do not forget my law, But let your heart keep my commands; For length of days and long life And peace they will add to you. Let not mercy and truth forsake you; Bind them around your neck, Write them on the tablet of your heart, And so find favor and high esteem In the sight of God and man.

Solomon encouraged his audience, in Proverbs 3:1–4, to dutifully study God's Word, observe it, and remain loyal to it, for at that time they will experience favor with God and man. Once a Christian adheres to the will, word, and ways of God, success is guaranteed to come. The Bible declares it.

Psalm 1 agrees with the notion: if a man walks and lives according to God's plan—success is bound to come.

> Psalm 1:1–3 (AMP)—*BLESSED (HAPPY, fortunate, prosperous, and enviable) is the man who walks and lives not in the counsel of the ungodly [following their advice, their plans and purposes], nor stands [submissive and inactive] in the path where sinners walk, nor sits down [to relax and rest] where the scornful [and the mockers] gather. But his delight and desire are in the law of the Lord, and on His law (the precepts, the instructions, the teachings of God) he habitually meditates (ponders and studies) by day and by night. And he shall be like a tree firmly planted [and tended] by the streams of water, ready to bring forth its fruit in its season; its leaf also shall not fade or wither; and everything he does shall prosper [and come to maturity].*

The apostle John's prayer in 3 John 1:2 seems to support the same notion.

> 3 John 1:2 (AMP)—*Beloved, I pray that you may prosper in every way and [that your body] may keep well, even as [I know] your soul keeps well and prospers.*

In the sixth chapter of Matthew, Jesus encouraged His followers not to worry too much about physical necessities, such as life, food, drink, body, and clothes. His rationale for not worrying was twofold. First He explained that worrying will not impact the situation or evoke change. Second He insinuated that the worldly thing ("these things") will come as a result of making God the center of your life.

> Matthew 6:33 (NKJV)—*But seek first the kingdom of God and His righteousness, and all these things shall be added to you.*

As I mentioned earlier, it is from walking in biblical happiness, the blessed state of making God the center of your life, that you will be able to successfully face life in every arena. The best verse to exemplify this fact is Psalm 23:6. It is here David wrote of the blessedness of being happy in the care of God, his Shepherd. He painted the picture of a believer's life that is secure in the Master's hands.

> Psalms 23:6—*Surely goodness and mercy shall follow me all the days of my life: and I will dwell in the house of the LORD for ever.*

Questions to Ask and Answer

1. Which of the four truths is more captivating to you? Why?

2. Why does the world fail to understand biblical happiness?

3. Should you base your happiness on your surroundings or happenings? Why?

4. What is the primary attribute needed to make God "happy" and position oneself for happiness? Explain. (Read Hebrews 11:6; Proverbs 16:7.)

5. Is the world's happiness and biblical happiness the same? What is the difference?

6. According to the Bible, does success or happiness come first? Support your answer.

Chapter 2

Truths You Should Know

Memory Verse: John 8:32 (BBE)—*And you will have knowledge of what is true, and that will make you free.*

1. List the four truths about true happiness covered in this book.

_____

_____

_____

_____

2. Knowing true happiness is not always perceived by the world as "happiness," list several ways you can prevent yourself from being distracted by the negativity of others.

_____

_____

3. Why is it so important for you to avoid distraction?

_____

_____

4. Reflect on the thought, "True success will never be achieved unless you attain true happiness."

_____

_____

5. The world is notorious for equating happy and successful Christians with materialism and greed; but what is the very foundation for a Christian's happiness and success?

_____

_____

6. Describe an instance when your happiness waned because you based it upon your feelings and perceptions only to discover that your predicament was not as bad as you perceived.

_____

_____

7. Read Romans 4:11–21 (note verse 18) aloud. Describe Abraham's belief system—was it based on visual appearances or faith in the spoken word of God?

_____

_____

8. Describe how your life would change if your happiness was totally based upon your faith in the spoken word of God.

_____

_____

_____

_____

9. Review the table below and reflect on the differences between worldly happiness and biblical happiness.

Worldly Happiness	**Biblical Happiness**
Physically rooted	Spiritually rooted
Based upon visual appearances, audible words, or emotional hunches	Based upon faith in God Almighty
Sees materialism and self-gratification as the source	Sees God Almighty as the only real, true, and reasonable source
Comes after success	Comes before success
Encourages pride and boastfulness	Encourages humility and selflessness
Makes you happy first	Makes God happy first

What other differences can you think of?

_____

_____

10. Reflect and write your thoughts about your life, your happiness, and your desire to be happy.

_____

_____

_____

_____

_____

_____

11. Write a detailed plan on how you will apply the truths discussed in this chapter into your life. Please include specific and immediate plans for implementation into your daily life.

_____

_____

_____

_____

_____

_____

_____

_____

Chapter 3

The Biblical Meaning of the Word "Happy"

And Leah said, I am happy, for women will call me blessed (happy, fortunate, to be envied); and she named him Asher [happy].
Genesis 30:13 (AMP)

When searching for the most accurate definition of biblical happiness, two languages should be considered: Hebrew and Greek. Within this chapter, I want to consider the main Hebrew and Greek words used in the Bible for happy: *esher* and *makarios*.

Esher

The word "*esher*" is used forty-five times in the Old Testament. The agreed upon meaning of the word is "blessed, happy, and to be envied." Basically this word implies the state of prosperity or happiness that comes when a superior bestows his favor (blessing) on one. In most passages, the one bestowing favor is God Himself.

The use of this word is spread throughout the Old Testament with the majority being in the poetry books. It is used one time in the books of law, four times in the books of history, thirty-six times in the books of poetry, and four times in the prophetic books.

Makarios

The word "*makarios*" is used fifty times in the New Testament.

The agreed upon meaning of the word is "supremely blessed, happy, fortunate, well off, and in position." Basically this word implies fortunate or blessed. In most passages, the one bestowing special favor or pronouncement is God Himself.

The use of this word is spread throughout the New Testament with the majority being in the gospels. It is used thirty times in the gospels, two times in the book of history, eleven times in the letters, and seven times in the book of prophecy.

It is evident the Bible has much to reveal on the subject of happiness. The Bible overwhelmingly describes being happy as being blessed, fortunate, and prosperous. Therefore, for the sake of clarity, as this book is concerned, one who is biblically happy is "blessed, happy, fortunate, well off, in position, and to be envied." A biblically happy person has an internal state of blessedness and happiness that transcends all external conditions of life.

Paul alluded to this blessed state as he compared their physical state to their spiritual state.

> 2 Corinthians 4:8–9 (NKJV)—*We are hard pressed on every side, yet not crushed; we are perplexed, but not in despair; persecuted, but not forsaken; struck down, but not destroyed.*

> 2 Corinthians 4:16 (MSG)—*So we're not giving up. How could we! Even though on the outside it often looks like things are falling apart on us, on the inside, where God is making new life, not a day goes by without his unfolding grace.*

On another occasion Paul referred to this state of happiness and how it transcended external conditions of life.

> 2 Corinthians 12:9–10 (NKJV)—*And He said to me, "My grace is sufficient for you, for My strength is made perfect*

in weakness." Therefore most gladly I will rather boast in my infirmities, that the power of Christ may rest upon me. Therefore I take pleasure in infirmities, in reproaches, in needs, in persecutions, in distresses, for Christ's sake. For when I am weak, then I am strong.

On both occasions Paul maintained a state of happiness despite the "happenings" occurring in his life. It is fully possible and biblical for you to operate in happiness while experiencing trials and tribulations in your life.

Consider the very words of Jesus to his dismal disciples:

John 16:33 (NKJV)—*These things I have spoken to you, that in Me you may have peace. In the world you will have tribulation; but be of good cheer, I have overcome the world.*

James also spoke of the ability to have happiness and joy in the midst of various trials. His conclusion was perception. When a Christian understands the purposes of trials—increased faith, patience and perfection—they can be happy and rejoice despite the circumstances.

James 1:2–4 (NIV)—*Consider it pure joy, my brothers, whenever you face trials of many kinds, because you know that the testing of your faith develops perseverance. Perseverance must finish its work so that you may be mature and complete, not lacking anything.*

Jeremiah even alluded to this divine happy state that is fully possible regardless of external conditions of life.

Lamentations 3:19–23 (AMP)—*[O Lord] remember [earnestly] my affliction and my misery, my wandering and my outcast state, the wormwood and the gall. My soul has them continually in remembrance and is bowed down within me. But this I recall and therefore have I hope and expectation: It is because of the Lord's mercy and loving-kindness that we are not consumed, because His [tender] compassions fail not. They are new every morning; great and abundant is Your stability and faithfulness.*

In Lamentations, chapter 3, Jeremiah confessed his continuous battles with depression and despair; but he refused to allow his external conditions to dictate his internal state, his God-given right to be happy. In so many words, I can hear Jeremiah shouting, *I am still blessed, happy, fortunate, well off, in position and to be envied—despite my present-day battles!*

What about you? Have you made up your mind and fixed your heart to walk in the happiness of God? Do you realize that happiness is God's gift to you? As you observe the abundance of scriptures pertaining to your happiness, it is my prayer that you will begin to accept the happiness of God and diligently strive to walk in it.

Questions to Ask and Answer

1. What is the best way to describe a biblically happy person?

2. Is the subject of happiness thoroughly discussed in the Bible? Explain your rationale.

3. Is it realistically possible to be happy despite storms, disappointments, shortfalls, and tribulations? How?

4. What lessons can be learned about biblical happiness despite external disaster? (Read Habakkuk 3:17–19.)

5. In what ways can you relate your personal testimony to the words of Habakkuk, Paul, Jeremiah, and James?

6. What steps have you taken to walk in the happiness of God?

Chapter 3

The Biblical Meaning of the Word "Happy"

Memory Verse: Genesis 30:13 (AMP)—*And Leah said, I am happy, for women will call me blessed (happy, fortunate, to be envied); and she named him Asher [happy].*

1. The Hebrew word for happy is "esher." What is the agreed upon meaning of this word?

_____

_____

2. How many times is this word used in the Old Testament?

_____

3. The Greek word for happy is "makarios." What is the agreed upon meaning of this word?

_____

Realizing Happiness

4. How many times is this word used in the New Testament?

_____

5. Reflect on the thought, "True happiness is an internal state of blessedness and happiness that transcends all external conditions of life." What are your immediate thoughts?

_____

_____

_____

_____

This suggest that I should: _____

_____

_____

6. Read 2 Corinthians 4:8–18 and 2 Corinthians 12:7–10 aloud. Describe Paul's plight in each instance.

_____

_____

_____

Describe how his responses exemplify true happiness.

_____

_____

_____

The Biblical Meaning of the Word "Happy"

7. Read Lamentations 3:1–26 aloud. Describe Jeremiah's plight.

_____

_____

_____

Describe how his response exemplifies true happiness.

_____

_____

_____

8. Paul and Jeremiah—despite their troubling conditions—made a decision to walk in true happiness. Spend a moment reflecting on areas within your life that are troubling; then list them.

_____

_____

_____

Now make the decision to rise above your conditions and walk in true happiness (cross them out).

_____

_____

_____

_____

9. Reflect and write your thoughts on the following questions: What about you? Have you made up your mind and fixed your heart to walk in the happiness of God? Do you realize that happiness is God's gift to you?

_____

_____

_____

_____

_____

_____

_____

_____

_____

_____

_____

_____

_____

_____

Chapter 4

God Wants You To Be Happy

For I know the plans I have for you, declares the LORD, plans to prosper you and not to harm you, plans to give you hope and a future.
Jeremiah 29:11 (NIV)

Modern society has several adages in which it lives by; however, the state of biblical happiness is not reached by selfishly pursuing the world's standards of happiness and following its wisdom.

It is accomplished by two things:

1. The gracious and merciful work of God Almighty on our behalf.

2. The faithful and unwavering devotion of an individual to please God Almighty by walking in His perfect will.

In the next chapter, I will examine the latter. But in this chapter, I wish to examine the gracious and merciful work of God Almighty on our behalf. I want to exclude you and your responsibility in achieving happiness while observing God and His commitment to your achieving happiness.

Prepare yourself for what I am about to say. God wants you to be happy. His desire is for you to live in—and even die in—a state of blessedness and happiness.

> Revelation 14:13 (AMP)—*Then I heard further [perceiving the distinct words of] a voice from heaven, saying, Write this: Blessed (happy, to be envied) are the dead from now on who die in the Lord! Yes, blessed (happy, to be envied indeed), says the Spirit, [in] that they may rest from their labors, for their works (deeds) do follow (attend, accompany) them!*

The commitment of God stretches wide covering a vast diversity of people.

> John 3:16 (NKJV)—*For God so loved the world that He gave His only begotten Son, that whoever believes in Him should not perish but have everlasting life.*

The common denominator that links each of us together is our willingness to accept His grace and mercy. God has promised an abundance of life to those who believe in His Son, Jesus. For the Christian it is difficult to not experience happiness. As Christians we live by faith not by sight, so our happiness is linked to our reliance on God. "The just shall live by faith" (Rom. 1:17). This is why we are able to rejoice and be thankful always because we are stimulated by more than external situations.

There are three commitments God has made to secure our happiness.

He chooses and calls us.

> Psalms 65:4 (AMP)—*Blessed (happy, fortunate, to be envied) is the man whom You choose and cause to come near, that he may dwell in Your courts! We shall be satisfied with the goodness of Your house, Your holy temple.*

The Psalmist regarded the priests who were chosen and called of God to minister at the tabernacle as happy. Though we are not Old Testament priests, we are a kingdom of priests, chosen and called by God to offer Him praise and worship; therefore, we also experience a state of divine happiness.

> 1 Peter 2:9–10 (AMP)—*But you are a chosen race, a royal priesthood, a dedicated nation, [God's] own purchased, special people, that you may set forth the wonderful deeds and display the virtues and perfections of Him Who called you out of darkness into His marvelous light. Once you were not a people [at all], but now you are God's people; once you were unpitied, but now you are pitied and have received mercy.*

> Revelation 1:6—*And hath made us kings and priests unto God and his Father; to him be glory and dominion for ever and ever. Amen.*

God in His infinite wisdom before the very foundations of the world wanted us to experience a state of true happiness, so He chose and called us.

> Ephesians 1:4 (AMP)—*Even as [in His love] He chose us [actually picked us out for Himself as His own] in Christ before the foundation of the world, that we should be holy (consecrated and set apart for Him) and blameless in His sight, even above reproach, before Him in love.*

> John 15:16 (AMP)—*You have not chosen Me, but I have chosen you and I have appointed you [I have planted you], that you might go and bear fruit and keep on bearing, and that your fruit may be lasting [that it may remain, abide], so that whatever you ask the Father in My Name [as presenting all that I AM], He may give it to you.*

He forgives, covers, and relieves us

> Psalms 32:1–2 (AMP)—*BLESSED (HAPPY, fortunate, to be envied) is he who has forgiveness of his transgression*

> continually exercised upon him, whose sin is covered. Blessed (happy, fortunate, to be envied) is the man to whom the Lord imputes no iniquity and in whose spirit there is no deceit.

God understands the sins and imperfections of man better than anyone. He created us in His own image. Sin, however, has crept into the world and distorted every facet of life because of the fall of Adam.

> Romans 5:12 (AMP)—*Therefore, as sin came into the world through one man, and death as the result of sin, so death spread to all men, [no one being able to stop it or to escape its power] because all men sinned.*

> Jeremiah 17:9 (AMP)—*The heart is deceitful above all things, and it is exceedingly perverse and corrupt and severely, mortally sick! Who can know it [perceive, understand, be acquainted with his own heart and mind]?*

Even though Adam sinned and jeopardized the God-desired happiness for our lives, God had a plan for our salvation and placed it in motion to redeem us from the clutches of sin and restore us to a state of happiness.

> Romans 5:18 (AMP)—*Well then, as one man's trespass [one man's false step and falling away led] to condemnation for all men, so one Man's act of righteousness [leads] to acquittal and right standing with God and life for all men.*

> Galatians 4:4–5 (NIV)—*But when the time had fully come, God sent his Son, born of a woman, born under law, to redeem those under law, that we might receive the full rights of sons.*

It is in this gracious act of Almighty God—the sacrifice of His

Son—that our happiness is found. Happy is he who is forgiven, covered, and relieved. This is exactly what God has done for the Christian: He has forgiven our transgression. He has covered our sin. He has relieved our iniquity. And God has done this because of His love for us and His desire for us to walk in a true state of happiness. Yes, God wants you to be happy! You are blessed!

As Paul argued the issue of "justification by faith" to the Romans, he referred to the God-desired state of happiness for the Jews and the Gentiles. His conclusion is revealing: *the God-desired happiness is for all who are justified by faith!*

> Romans 4:6–9 (AMP)—*Thus David congratulates the man and pronounces a blessing on him to whom God credits righteousness apart from the works he does: Blessed and happy and to be envied are those whose iniquities are forgiven and whose sins are covered up and completely buried. Blessed and happy and to be envied is the person of whose sin the Lord will take no account nor reckon it against him. Is this blessing (happiness) then meant only for the circumcised, or also for the uncircumcised? We say that faith was credited to Abraham as righteousness.*

He disciplines and instructs us

> Job 5:17 (AMP)—*Happy and fortunate is the man whom God reproves; so do not despise or reject the correction of the Almighty [subjecting you to trial and suffering].*

> Psalms 94:12 (AMP)—*Blessed (happy, fortunate, to be envied) is the man whom You discipline and instruct, O Lord, and teach out of Your law…*

One of the greatest signs of love in parenthood is discipline. A father or mother who will reprove their children to empower and develop them into better individuals is noteworthy. God has been so gracious to Christians. He has chosen and called us; forgiven, covered, and relieved us; and now in His infinite love is willing to continuously rear us. So that we may be conformed into the image of His Son, Jesus the Christ, God has committed Himself to leading us in the paths of righteousness for His name's sake (Ps. 23:3).

Why is God so dedicated to you receiving the proper nurture and provision? I believe the answer is simple: God wants you to be happy. Jesus declared, in John 10:10, that life for the believer should be abundant. The Bible declares blessed, happy, fortunate, well off, in position, and envied is the man whom the Lord cares enough about to discipline and instruct.

> Proverbs 3:11–12 (AMP)—*My son, do not despise or shrink from the chastening of the Lord [His correction by punishment or by subjection to suffering or trial]; neither be weary of or impatient about or loathe or abhor His reproof, For whom the Lord loves He corrects, even as a father corrects the son in whom he delights.*

In the twenty-third Psalm, David gave a beautiful picture of the life of a believer who is willing to receive the discipline and instruction of God. The most noteworthy point made by the Psalmist is that the Shepherd is more than willing to love, care, protect, and make happy the sheep of His pasture. David concluded the Psalm by implying that the sheep understand the importance of never leaving the Shepherd's presence.

God's commitment to Christians is remarkable. He has clearly demonstrated His willingness to position us in a state of happiness. Will you receive it? Will you walk in it? Will you remain in His presence? God has chosen and called you to happiness. He is continually forgiving, covering, relieving, disciplining, and instructing you so you can be happy. As far as God is concerned, *you should be happy*!

Psalm 103:2–5 (MSG)—*O my soul, bless God, don't forget a single blessing! He forgives your sins—every one. He heals your diseases—every one. He redeems you from hell—saves your life! He crowns you with love and mercy—a paradise crown. He wraps you in goodness—beauty eternal. He renews your youth—you are always young in his presence. God makes everything come out right; he puts victims back on their feet.*

Hebrews 13:5–6 (MSG)—*Don't be obsessed with getting more material things. Be relaxed with what you have. Since God assured us, "I'll never let you down, never walk off and leave you," we can boldly quote, God is there, ready to help; I'm fearless no matter what. Who or what can get to me?*

Questions to Ask and Answer

1. How is biblical happiness accomplished in comparison to worldly happiness?

2. Does God truly want you to be happy? Explain.

3. What are the three ways in which God has positioned you to be happy?

4. Do you feel chosen and called? Why?

5. Have your sins been forgiven and covered? (Read John 3:16; 1 John 1:9.)

6. How does it make you feel to know that God is disciplining and instructing you for your own edification? Are you willing to humble yourself? Why?

7. Has God provided an ample avenue for true happiness? Are you interested? Explain.

Chapter 4

God Wants You To Be Happy

Memory Verse: Jeremiah 29:11 (NIV)—*For I know the plans I have for you, declares the LORD, plans to prosper you and not to harm you, plans to give you hope and a future.*

1. True happiness is accomplished by what two things?
_____
_____

2. List the three commitments God made to secure our happiness?
_____
_____
_____
_____

God Wants You To Be Happy

3. Read Psalm 65:4 and 1 Peter 2:9–10 aloud. Describe the correlation between God's chosen and called priests in the Old Testament and His chosen and called kingdom of priests in the New Testament. (Read Ephesians 1:4; John 15:16.)

_____

_____

_____

_____

4. Read Psalm 32:1–2 and Romans 4:6–9 aloud. Explain why you feel God has so graciously forgiven, covered, and relieved the "household of faith."

_____

_____

_____

_____

5. How do you perceive God's willingness to reprove, chasten, and discipline His own. Do you see it as positive, negative, or both?

_____

_____

_____

_____

6. Read Proverbs 3:11–12 aloud. Describe Solomon's perception of the Lord's chastening. What does he compare it to?

_____

_____

7. Read Job 5:17 and Psalms 94:12 aloud. Describe the end results of God's love to those He chastens.

_____

_____

8. Review the table below and reflect on the scriptural evidence of God's commitment to your happiness.

God's Commitment to Your Happiness	Scripture Reference
He chose and called you	Psalm 65:4; 1 Peter 2:9-10; Revelations 1:6; Ephesians 1:4; John 15:16
He forgave, covered, and relieved you	Psalm 32:1-2; Romans 4:6-9
He disciplines and instructs us	Job 5:17; Psalm 94:12

Are you convinced? If not, what is hindering you?

_____

_____

_____

_____

Chapter 5

Happiness Can Be Yours

Be happy with the LORD, and he will give you the desires of your heart.
Psalm 37:4 (GW)

The state of happiness is accomplished by two things:

1. The gracious and merciful work of God Almighty on our behalf.

2. The faithful unwavering devotion an individual has to pleasing God Almighty by walking in His perfect will.

In the previous chapter, I explored three areas of God's gracious and merciful work on your behalf. Now I am going to explore several scriptures that guarantee your happiness if you walk in the will of God.

Do you want to be happy? Do you want a state of being that transcends your everyday situations and circumstances? Do you want to remain happy even during times of worldly unhappiness (e.g. unemployment, war, sickness, recession, etc.)? Are you ready to be able to say with confidence, *"I'm blessed—I'm supremely happy!"*? Well, put on your spiritual walking shoes.

Make Jesus LORD

1 Peter 5:6 (NIV)—*Humble yourselves, therefore, under*

God's mighty hand, that he may lift you up in due time.

One of the first things a person should do is humble himself or herself before the Lord. As Christians we have accomplished one of the greatest feats in the history of mankind. Salvation has become a living reality for each of us. We have made Jesus our Savior! God has rescued us from the pits of hell and assured us the promise of eternal life. Such a life is great but not complete. Jesus Christ did not come to earth and die just so we can go to heaven someday. He also came to destroy the works of the devil and to be the sole example of our destiny.

> 1 John 3:8—*He that committeth sin is of the devil; for the devil sinneth from the beginning. For this purpose the Son of God was manifested, that he might destroy the works of the devil.*

> Romans 8:29—*For whom he did foreknow, he also did predestinate to be conformed to the image of his Son, that he might be the firstborn among many brethren.*

The phraseology used to describe this understanding of being conformed to His image is "making Jesus Lord." Have you made Jesus the Lord of your life? When Christians allow Jesus to be Lord, they position themselves for happiness. The Bible is clear, "The steps of a good man are ordered by the LORD: and he delighteth in his way" (Ps. 37:23).

The sheep represented in Psalm 23 are extremely blessed, satisfied, and happy. Essentially the Shepherd is the ruler and decision maker. David wrote of at least six acts the Shepherd does for the sheep without question. The Shepherd makes, leads, restores, protects, prepares, and anoints the sheep solely for the sheep's best interest.

In John 10, Jesus referred to Himself as the Good Shepherd. So when you recognize Jesus as the Good Shepherd, you, in essence, acknowledge Him as Lord. He becomes your God thus positioning you to enjoy happiness.

> Psalm 144:15 (AMP)—*Happy and blessed are the people who are in such a case; yes, happy (blessed, fortunate, prosperous, to be envied) are the people whose God is the Lord!*

Solely depend on God

The foundation of Christianity is faith. Paul, in his letter to the Romans, repeatedly made this claim clear.

> Romans 3:28—*Therefore we conclude that a man is justified by faith without the deeds of the law.*

> Romans 1:17—*For therein is the righteousness of God revealed from faith to faith: as it is written, The just shall live by faith.*

Paul asserted that a Christian's start and survival are predicated on faith. Faith is an unwavering dependence on God Almighty to provide, protect, and preserve. The Bible promises to place Christians in a state of happiness if they will solely depend on God.

> Psalms 34:8 (AMP)—*O taste and see that the Lord [our God] is good! Blessed (happy, fortunate, to be envied) is the man who trusts and takes refuge in Him.*

> Psalms 40:4 (AMP)—*Blessed (happy, fortunate, to be envied) is the man who makes the Lord his refuge and trust, and turns not to the proud or to followers of false gods.*

> John 20:29 (AMP)—*Jesus said to him, Because you have seen Me, Thomas, do you now believe (trust, have faith)?*

Blessed and happy and to be envied are those who have never seen Me and yet have believed and adhered to and trusted and relied on Me.

Proverbs 16:20 (AMP)—*He who deals wisely and heeds [God's] word and counsel shall find good, and whoever leans on, trusts in, and is confident in the Lord—happy, blessed, and fortunate is he.*

Psalms 146:5 (AMP)—*Happy (blessed, fortunate, enviable) is he who has the God of [special revelation to] Jacob for his help, whose hope is in the Lord his God...*

Psalms 2:12 (AMP)—*Kiss the Son [pay homage to Him in purity], lest He be angry and you perish in the way, for soon shall His wrath be kindled. O blessed (happy, fortunate, and to be envied) are all those who seek refuge and put their trust in Him!*

You will be happy if you make a conscious decision today to rely on God for your provision, protection, and preservation. Doubt is one of the chief reasons why many Christians live defeated, unhappy lives. They trust God enough to save them from their sins, but they do not trust Him enough in their everyday lives.

James 1:6–8 (NKJV)—*But let him ask in faith, with no doubting, for he who doubts is like a wave of the sea driven and tossed by the wind. For let not that man suppose that he will receive anything from the Lord; he is a double-minded man, unstable in all his ways.*

Solomon encouraged believers to always trust God with their total being. His theory is to never rely on your own understanding. Too much is at stake when you do, namely your happiness.

Proverbs 3:5 (AMP)—*Lean on, trust in, and be confident*

in the Lord with all your heart and mind and do not rely on your own insight or understanding.

Find wisdom and get understanding

Ephesians 2:8 (AMP)—*For it is by free grace (God's unmerited favor) that you are saved (delivered from judgment and made partakers of Christ's salvation) through [your] faith. And this [salvation] is not of yourselves [of your own doing, it came not through your own striving], but it is the gift of God.*

When a person becomes a Christian, it is based on their faith. From that point in time, there is a lot to learn and discover about the Christian journey. Therefore, there must be a determination to learn and discover more about God and His kingdom. It is in the pursuit of God that Christians find happiness.

Proverbs 3:13 (AMP)—*Happy (blessed, fortunate, enviable) is the man who finds skillful and godly Wisdom, and the man who gets understanding [drawing it forth from God's Word and life's experiences].*

In his writings Paul repeatedly encouraged Christians to flee mere human wisdom and seek the spiritual things of God.

Colossians 2:20 (AMP)—*If then you have died with Christ to material ways of looking at things and have escaped from the world's crude and elemental notions and teachings of externalism, why do you live as if you still belong to the world.*

Colossians 3:2 (AMP)—*Set your minds and keep them set on what is above (the higher things), not on the things that are on the earth.*

2 Corinthians 10:3–5 (NIV)—*For though we live in the*

> world, we do not wage war as the world does.

> 1 Corinthians 2:5 (AMP)—*So that your faith might not rest in the wisdom of men (human philosophy), but in the power of God.*

> 2 Timothy 2:15—*Study to shew thyself approved unto God, a workman that needeth not to be ashamed, rightly dividing the word of truth.*

Fear God

To fear God means to develop a sincere reverence for Him which includes enough respect to honor His hatred of sin in your life. This reverence and respect should be the motivating factor for you to surrender and humble yourself under the mighty hand of God.

> Hebrews 12:28–29 (AMP)—*Let us therefore, receiving a kingdom that is firm and stable and cannot be shaken, offer to God pleasing service and acceptable worship, with modesty and pious care and godly fear and awe; For our God [is indeed] a consuming fire.*

When Christians are keenly aware of the awesome presence of God "in and on" their lives, it produces a heartfelt worship within them that transcends outwardly. In Psalm 103 David exemplified the fear of the Lord when he shouted, "Blessed (praise) the Lord, my total being, all that is within me—praise the Lord!" When you reverence God to this extent, you can expect two definite things to happen: you will begin to walk according to the will of God, and you will find yourself in an unbelievable state of happiness. You will be happy—anyhow, regardless, and despite.

> Psalms 112:1 (AMP)—*PRAISE THE Lord! (Hallelujah!) Blessed (happy, fortunate, to be envied) is the man who fears (reveres and worships) the Lord, who delights*

greatly in His commandments.

Psalms 128:1 (AMP)—BLESSED (HAPPY, fortunate, to be envied) is everyone who fears, reveres, and worships the Lord, who walks in His ways and lives according to His commandments.

Proverbs 28:14 (AMP)—Blessed (happy, fortunate, and to be envied) is the man who reverently and worshipfully fears [the Lord] at all times [regardless of circumstances], but he who hardens his heart will fall into calamity.

I am convinced that happiness flows from heartfelt worship and reverence of God. The New Testament spends a great deal of time encouraging believers to stay focused on God's provisions and retain the proper perspective on life's situations. The apostle Paul wrote heavily on the need to rejoice always, give thanks in everything, and pray without ceasing. Why? Because he understood the impact it has on our happiness.

David's writings seem to support this philosophy. He wrote, in Psalm 34, "I will bless the Lord at all times, and His praise will continually be in my mouth." His attitude seems to exemplify the life of a believer who is striving to be happy.

Do not be offended

As difficult as it may sound, everyone was not excited or enthused with Jesus' teaching and preaching. Many considered His style to be offensive and nontraditional. He did not attempt to patronize with the religious leaders or sugarcoat His message for the unsaved. His delivery was God-ordained.

John 5:30 (NKJV)—I can of Myself do nothing. As I hear, I judge; and My judgment is righteous, because I do not seek My own will but the will of the Father who sent Me.

Contempt for the Word of God aroused for various reasons. In Luke 4:22, after Jesus completed His reading of the Book of Isaiah, the community became baffled that Jesus—the son of Joseph—could impact them as He did. Once the Pharisees discovered what He did (v.28), they were full of wrath because He was outshining them in the community. Their response was to thrust Him out of the city (v.29).

Jesus' disciples even reached a point in their walk when they questioned his thoughts and actions. He became so offensive that the majority of His disciples—except the twelve—walked away from Him (John 6:66). The twelve resorted to remaining by His side after He questioned them.

Matthew 11:6 (AMP)—*And blessed (happy, fortunate, and to be envied) is he who takes no offense at Me and finds no cause for stumbling in or through Me and is not hindered from seeing the Truth.*

In Matthew 11:6 Jesus made an astounding remark to the surrounding listeners. John the Baptist had sent two of his disciples to Jesus questioning Him of His calling. In response to John, He declared miracles are still taking place (v.5). But to the multitude, He gives an open invitation to happiness. Happy is the person who walks in the truth without stumbling.

Endure temptation

One of the greatest challenges of living the Christian life is approaching and properly managing temptation. For example, it can be very disappointing for someone to know that his sins have been forgiven only to immediately find himself bombarded by temptation that seek to cause him to sin again. Every Christian experiences temptation.

The apostle Paul alluded to this fact, when writing to the Corinthians, in 1 Corinthians 10:12–13 (MSG): "Don't be so naive and self-confident. You're not exempt. You could fall flat on your face as easily as anyone else." Peter agreed when he wrote, "Beloved, do not think it strange concerning the fiery trial which is to try you, as though some strange thing happened to you" (Pet. 4:12 NKJV). Temptation is a part of the Christian life. It is inevitable to each and every child of God.

Temptation haunts us at every age. It riddles us as children, devastates us as adolescents, and confuses us as adults; so much, we live our lives in conflict. The biggest mistake is to deny that temptation exists. Victory is found in accepting the inevitable—and "fighting the good fight of faith" (1 Tim. 6:12).

The apostle Paul has encouraged Christians throughout the ages to be strong in the Lord. Repeatedly he suggested that it was the only way for believers to survive in the midst of spiritual warfare. In 2 Timothy 2:3 (NKJV) we are instructed to "endure hardship as a good soldier of Jesus Christ." Happiness is guaranteed to those who endure temptation as good soldiers. Facing warfare as soldiers who are fully equipped and armed and ready to patiently stand "in the midst of a crooked and perverse generation, among whom you shine as lights in the world" (Phil. 2:15 NKJV).

> James 1:12 (AMP)—*Blessed (happy, to be envied) is the man who is patient under trial and stands up under temptation.*

Questions to Ask and Answer

1. Are you convinced that happiness can be yours?

2. What is the most compelling factor that lead you to your decision?

3. To what degree do you play in your happiness?

4. Name the ways mentioned in this chapter that you can walk in happiness.

5. Which way(s) do you have the most confidence in?

6. Which way(s) do you find the most challenging?

7. What can you do to improve your walk in the areas where you most struggle?

8. Stop! Make a list of objectives and goals that will strengthen your walk and increase your happiness.

Chapter 5

Happiness Can Be Yours

Memory Verse: Psalms 37:4 (GW)—*Be happy with the LORD, and he will give you the desires of your heart.*

1. The state of happiness is accomplished by two things. What is the second thing?

_____

_____

2. After reading about the reality of happiness and how it is heavily dependent on your Christian walk, describe your commitment and dedication to making happiness yours.

_____

_____

_____

3. Define "humble," then explain it in the context of 1 Peter 5:6.

_____

_____

4. What are some traits of a Christian who has made Jesus Lord?

_____

_____

5. According to Psalms 23, what are the six acts that the Shepherd does for His sheep?

_____

_____

These acts are freely administered by the Shepherd because the sheep freely allow Him to be the Shepherd. Apply this same concept to your life. What can you expect from the Lord if you wholeheartedly allow Him to be the Lord of your life?

_____

_____

6. According to Romans 1:17, "the just shall live by faith." What is your understanding of the word "live"? What images come to mind?

_____

_____

_____

Happiness Can Be Yours

7. Review the table below. How do the verses listed describe the life of one who lives by faith.

Scripture Reference	Description of "A Life Lived by Faith"
Psalm 34:8 (AMP)—O taste and see that the Lord [our God] is good! Blessed (happy, fortunate, to be envied) is the man who trusts and takes refuge in Him.	Blessed, happy, fortunate, to be envied
Psalm 40:4 (AMP)—Blessed (happy, fortunate, to be envied) is the man who makes the Lord his refuge and trust, and turns not to the proud or to followers of false gods.	Blessed, happy, fortunate, to be envied
Proverbs 16:20 (AMP)—He who deals wisely and heeds [God's] word and counsel shall find good, and whoever leans on, trusts in, and is confident in the Lord—happy, blessed, and fortunate is he.	Blessed, happy, fortunate
Psalms 146:5 (AMP)—Happy (blessed, fortunate, enviable) is he who has the God of [special revelation to] Jacob for his help, whose hope is in the Lord his God...	Blessed, happy, fortunate, enviable
Psalms 2:12 (AMP)—Kiss the Son [pay homage to Him in purity], lest He be angry and you perish in the way, for soon shall His wrath be kindled. O blessed (happy, fortunate, and to be envied) are all those who seek refuge and put their trust in Him!	Blessed, happy, fortunate, to be envied
John 20:29 (AMP)—Jesus said to him, Because you have seen Me, Thomas, do you now believe (trust, have faith)? Blessed and happy and to be envied are those who have never seen Me and yet have believed and adhered to and trusted and relied on Me.	Blessed, happy, fortunate, to be envied

Are you convinced of the happiness that comes with faith? Why?

_____

_____

_____

8. Read 1 Corinthians 2:5, Colossians 2:20, and Romans 10:17 aloud. How important is it that our faith be based upon the Word of God and not rest in the wisdom of men? Why?

_____

_____

_____

_____

9. Explain what the phrase "fear God" means.

_____

_____

How can you apply the stated connotation to your personal life?

_____

_____

10. How often does the Word of God convict you of sins in your life? Are you offended or thankful?

_____

_____

What are the scriptural benefits for not taking offence to God and His Word?

_____

_____

Chapter 6

Happiness Can Be Yours - Part 2

Then shalt thou delight thyself in the LORD; and I will cause thee to ride upon the high places of the earth, and feed thee with the heritage of Jacob thy father: for the mouth of the LORD hath spoken it.
Isaiah 58:14

This chapter continues to explore several scriptures that guarantee your happiness if you walk in the will of God.

Be a doer of the word

Many people never achieve happiness because they are so imbalanced in their Christian walk. They learn how or strive to please God only in portions of His stated will. For example, God does promise to bless you and give you happiness if you trust Him, gain wisdom from Him, and fear Him; however, if you do those things only and fail to be obedient to Him in other areas—it is for naught.

> Luke 11:28 (AMP)—*But He said, Blessed (happy and to be envied) rather are those who hear the Word of God and obey and practice it!*

> Psalm 119:1–2 (AMP)—*BLESSED (HAPPY, fortunate, to be envied) are the undefiled (the upright, truly sincere, and blameless) in the way [of the revealed will of God], who walk (order their conduct and conversation) in the law of the Lord (the whole of God's revealed will). Blessed (happy, fortunate, to be envied) are they who keep His*

> testimonies, and who seek, inquire for and of Him and crave Him with the whole heart.

> Proverbs 29:18 (AMP)—*Where there is no vision [no redemptive revelation of God], the people perish; but he who keeps the law [of God, which includes that of man]—blessed (happy, fortunate, and enviable) is he.*

The Bible is unmistakable in its requirement that we must be "hearers and doers" of the Word to experience the fullness of God's kingdom. Mary, the mother of Jesus, has become known virtually by the fact that she was the chosen vessel of God to bear the Messiah. On one occasion, in Luke 11:27–28, a woman lifted up her voice to Jesus and said, *happy, blessed is your mother's womb because of you.* Jesus replied, *yes my mother is blessed, but those who hear and practice the Word of God are truly happy.*

It has been said that faith starts where the will of God is known. This statement implies that faith understands God's intents and adheres to them. As Christians desiring to maintain our God-given happiness, we must diligently search the Bible for direction and guidance. After the path has been charted, we must follow the Lord's steps, or we jeopardize our happiness.

> Romans 10:17—*So then faith cometh by hearing, and hearing by the word of God.*

> James 1:25 (NKJV)—*But he who looks into the perfect law of liberty and continues in it, and is not a forgetful hearer but a doer of the work, this one will be blessed in what he does.*

Walk in holiness

> Hebrews 12:14 (NIV)—*Make every effort to live in peace with all men and to be holy; without holiness no one will see the Lord.*

The culmination of a life lived trusting God, seeking His wisdom, respecting His character, and obeying His Word is a life of holiness. The writer of Hebrews shared his insights on how the Christian race should be run: peace with all men *and holiness* before the Lord. In some Christian circles and denominations, the concept of holiness has faded. To live holy has become taboo for some. Yet the Bible is clear on its position on holiness.

> Luke 1:74–75 (AMP)—*To grant us that we, being delivered from the hand of our foes, might serve Him fearlessly. In holiness (divine consecration) and righteousness [in accordance with the everlasting principles of right] within His presence all the days of our lives.*

Zacharias, having been stricken mute by an angel of God, remained silent throughout his wife's pregnancy. At the birth of his son, John (John the Baptist), Zacharias' voice was restored, and he began singing a song of praise to God for the forthcoming Messiah. In this song Zacharias tells of the importance of Jesus' advent. In Luke 1:74–75, he declares that the people of God will have total victory over the enemy, and in our deliverance we should serve God fearlessly—in holiness and righteousness. The reason God sent His Son to deliver us was so we could serve God in holiness.

> Romans 12:1 (NKJV)—*I beseech you therefore, brethren, by the mercies of God, that you present your bodies a living sacrifice, holy, acceptable to God, which is your reasonable service.*

Paul, as he concluded his theoretical discussion to the Romans, petitioned them to give of themselves wholeheartedly to the service of God. His words centered on their bodies, which, for far too long, they had used for sinful purposes. Paul shouted: *present them to God as living sacrifices, holy and acceptable. Holy!* God wants Christians to live *holy* lives. The Bible declares that God chose us before the foundation of the world to be holy and without blame.

> Ephesians 1:4 (NKJV)—*Just as He chose us in Him before the foundation of the world, that we should be holy and without blame before Him in love.*

In holiness you strive to live according to God's perfect will for your life; you refuse to "just live" or live according to His permissive will. Whether it is your marriage, employment, hobby, children, grandchildren, church, etc., your greatest objective in life should be to "do it God's way."

The Psalmist shared his thoughts on why he feels it is important to do it God's way.

> Psalms 18:30 (NKJV)—*As for God, His way is perfect; The word of the Lord is proven; He is a shield to all who trust in Him.*

In the midst of spiritual confusion and controversy, Joshua, God's chosen leader of Israel, in his old age, stated his heart's conviction—*my family and I will live lives of holiness!*

> Joshua 24:15—*And if it seem evil unto you to serve the LORD, choose you this day whom ye will serve; whether the gods which your fathers served that were on the other side of the flood, or the gods of the Amorites, in whose land ye dwell: but as for me and my house, we will serve the LORD.*

How important is it to you to live a life of holiness? Have you realized that your happiness is rooted in your everyday lifestyle? So how are you living? It had been said that Christianity is a way of life. If that is true, holiness and happiness should also be ways of life. Christians are called to be holy; and when they live lives of holiness, they will live lives of happiness.

Psalms 1:1 (AMP)—BLESSED (HAPPY, fortunate, prosperous, and enviable) is the man who walks and lives not in the counsel of the ungodly [following their advice, their plans and purposes], nor stands [submissive and inactive] in the path where sinners walk, nor sits down [to relax and rest] where the scornful [and the mockers] gather.

Psalms 119:1-2 (AMP)—BLESSED (HAPPY, fortunate, to be envied) are the undefiled (the upright, truly sincere, and blameless) in the way [of the revealed will of God], who walk (order their conduct and conversation) in the law of the Lord (the whole of God's revealed will). Blessed (happy, fortunate, to be envied) are they who keep His testimonies, and who seek, inquire for and of Him and crave Him with the whole heart.

Consider others

Another area to take into account is your kindness toward others. How do you honestly treat your neighbor? How often do you give to the benefit of others? This kindness goes beyond your tithes and offerings, church obligations, community commitments, career conditions, and organizational responsibilities. What do you do regularly for those who are less fortunate?

For many, happiness is a fleeting emotion because they fail to realize God's ultimate purpose for their lives. In the New Testament, Jesus spoke of only two commandments. The first demands holiness to God, and the second demands consideration to others. When was the last time you showed consideration to another person with no strings, responsibilities, or obligations attached? You did not have to, but you did "just because."

Psalm 106:3 (MSG)—You're one happy man when you do what's right, one happy woman when you form the habit of justice.

You can live in a state of happiness, but you must forget about yourself and consider your neighbor first. Trusting God to provide, protect, and preserve. The book of Psalms speaks to this glorious state when one considers others.

> Psalms 41:1 (AMP)—*BLESSED (HAPPY, fortunate, to be envied) is he who considers the weak and the poor; the Lord will deliver him in the time of evil and trouble.*

Solomon alluded to the same state of happiness which comes from loving, helping, supporting, blessing, and considering your neighbor first.

> Proverbs 14:21 (AMP)—*He who despises his neighbor sins [against God, his fellowman, and himself], but happy (blessed and fortunate) is he who is kind and merciful to the poor.*

To consider others is to go beyond the established boundaries of life to fulfill their needs. The Bible is prevalent in its descriptions and stories of people who went beyond what was required to help someone. In Luke 10:30–37, in response to the question "who is my neighbor?" Jesus told the story of a man who fell among thieves. He was bypassed by two likely people, a Levite and a Priest; neither thought enough of him to stop and help. The third person to approach the victim was a Samaritan, a person who was very unlikely to help. Yet the Bible says the Samaritan had compassion on the man. He truly considered the man, regardless of nationality.

In John 4:3–30 John told the story of Jesus having a conversation with a Samaritan woman. This story is so timely because in biblical culture Jews did not have any dealings with Samaritans—especially Jewish men and Samaritan women. But Jesus had compassion on this woman; He knew she needed His help. He truly considered the woman and helped her regardless of culture, gender, and lifestyle.

> John 13:17 (AMP)—*If you know these things, blessed and happy and to be envied are you if you practice them [if you act accordingly and really do them].*

In John 13:17 Jesus gave us another example of how our consideration for others should go beyond our mere comfort. Jesus, to the surprise of His disciples, washed each of their feet as a sign of love, respect, and humility. Jesus went as far as to say that the disciples should do the same one for another. The ultimate message is our love and consideration for others should transcend established or perceived titles, positions, and rights. He truly considered the disciples regardless of their titles, positions, and rights. Happiness is guaranteed when your consideration for others rises above class, nationality, gender, culture, title, position, rights, etc.

> *Acts 20:35 (MSG)—In everything I've done, I have demonstrated to you how necessary it is to work on behalf of the weak and not exploit them. You'll not likely go wrong here if you keep remembering that our Master said, 'You're far happier giving than getting.*

Wait on the Lord

The word "wait" is used in several contexts within the Bible. The most frequently used meaning of the word defines the proper attitude of a believer who is totally responsive to the voice and actions of God. It denotes the constant expectation of God to execute justice and mercy in due time.

The Bible is forthright about the benefits of "waiting on God." In Psalm 27:14 waiting will evoke God to strengthen weak hearts. In Psalm 37:9 waiting allows believers to inherit the earth. In Proverbs 20:22 waiting is the primary factor of deliverance.

Isaiah 40:31 is the most familiar verse concerning waiting. The prophet declared deliverance and restoration very much a reality. His primary emphasis was on "they that wait": those who refuse to look to the left or the right. It is this particular group that will receive strength, solace, endurance, and longsuffering.

With so many benefits, it is apparent a person who determines to place their focus on the Lord will be at peace and experience happiness. This person will spare themselves undue worries, distresses, and disappointments. Their mind-set becomes unusually settled with knowing God is in control despite external circumstances.

> Isaiah 30:18 (AMP)—*And therefore the Lord [earnestly] waits [expecting, looking, and longing] to be gracious to you; and therefore He lifts Himself up, that He may have mercy on you and show loving-kindness to you. For the Lord is a God of justice. Blessed (happy, fortunate, to be envied) are all those who [earnestly] wait for Him, who expect and look and long for Him [for His victory, His favor, His love, His peace, His joy, and His matchless, unbroken companionship]!*

Suffer for Christ's sake

The Bible is vivid in its discussion on persecution. Every Christian who faithfully carries out the will of God can expect to experience it in one form or fashion. In Psalm 34:19 (MSG) David concluded, "Disciples so often get into trouble." Trouble that manifests itself in various forms, such as, sufferings (Matt. 23:34–36), separation by excommunication (Jer. 12:9–11), reproaches (2 Chron. 36:16), and hatred (1 Kings 18:4).

In 1 Peter 3:17 Peter described two types of suffering: "For it is better, if it is the will of God, to suffer for doing good than for doing evil." Suffering for good offers numerous blessings for the recipients; this is contrary to suffering for evil. Persecution that arises from good produces perfection, stability, strength, and grounding for the believer (1 Pet. 5:10). This is why the apostle

Paul desired to be a partaker so much: "That I may know him…and the fellowship of his sufferings" (Phil. 3:10).

As Peter taught on the two types of suffering, he also taught on the two states of suffering. It is implied that a person who suffers for evil will reap the grim consequences of sadness. Contrarily it is stated that a believer who suffers for good will be happy.

> 1 Peter 3:14—*But and if ye suffer for righteousness' sake, happy are ye: and be not afraid of their terror, neither be troubled.*
>
> 1 Peter 4:14—*If ye be reproached for the name of Christ, happy are ye; for the spirit of glory and of God resteth upon you: on their part he is evil spoken of, but on your part he is glorified.*
>
> Matthew 5:10–11 (AMP)—*Blessed and happy and enviably fortunate and spiritually prosperous (in the state in which the born-again child of God enjoys and finds satisfaction in God's favor and salvation, regardless of his outward conditions) are those who are persecuted for righteousness' sake (for being and doing right), for theirs is the kingdom of heaven! Blessed (happy, to be envied, and spiritually prosperous—with life-joy and satisfaction in God's favor and salvation, regardless of your outward conditions) are you when people revile you and persecute you and say all kinds of evil things against you falsely on My account.*

Questions to Ask and Answer

1. After reading a vast amount of scriptures that center on the believer's happiness, are you convinced that happiness can be yours?

2. Has the most compelling factor that led you to your decision changed from your reply in the previous chapter?

3. In your opinion, once a person accepts God's plan for happiness, who is the most instrumental person in that believer's happiness? Why?

4. How does your answer in the last question relate to the age-old cliché: "You are your own worst enemy!"

5. Name the ways mentioned in this chapter that you can walk in happiness.

5. Which way(s) do you have the most confidence in?

6. Which way(s) do you find the most challenging?

7. What can you do to improve your walk in the areas where you most struggle?

8. Stop! Make a list of objectives and goals that will strengthen your walk and increase your happiness.

Chapter 6

Happiness Can Be Yours - Part 2

Memory Verse: Isaiah 58:14—*Then shalt thou delight thyself in the LORD; and I will cause thee to ride upon the high places of the earth, and feed thee with the heritage of Jacob thy father: for the mouth of the LORD hath spoken it.*

1. Dr. Turner said, "The Bible is very unmistakable in its requirement that we must be 'hearers and doers' of the Word to experience the fullness of God's kingdom." Spend a few moments reflecting on your Christian walk. What are your strengths, weaknesses, opportunities for growth, and threats to growth?

_____

_____

_____

_____

2. Dr. Turner said, "The culmination of a life lived trusting God, seeking His wisdom, respecting His character, and obeying His Word is a life of holiness." How important is it for you to live holy and acceptable before God?

_____

_____

How would you describe the correlation between living a life of holiness ("clean living") and being happy?

_____

_____

3. Acts 20:35 (MSG) says "You're far happier giving than getting." List at least three things you have done within the last month for someone else. How important is it to you to be kind and considerate to others?

_____

_____

_____

_____

What are some things that immediately come to mind when you pause and consider ways to be a blessing in the life of someone else?

_____

_____

Start implementing them today!

Happiness Can Be Yours - Part 2

4. Review the table below. Reflect on the benefits of waiting on the Lord.

_____

_____

Scripture Reference	Benefit of "Waiting on the Lord"
Psalm 27:14	Strength
Psalm 37:9	Inherit the earth
Proverbs 20:22	Deliverance
Isaiah 40:31	Strength, solace, endurance, and longsuffering

If you had everything the above table promised to those who wait on the Lord, how would that make you feel? What state does Isaiah 30:18 suggest?

5. Describe the two types of suffering mentioned in 1 Peter 3:17.

_____

_____

What are the two states of suffering discussed?

_____

_____

Which type of suffering seems the most rewarding?

_____

6. Reflect and write your thoughts on your commitment to being happy by walking in the will of God. Please include specific and immediate plans for implementation into your daily life.

_____
_____
_____
_____
_____
_____
_____
_____
_____
_____
_____
_____
_____
_____

Chapter 7

Your Character is Important

Moral character makes for smooth traveling; an evil life is a hard life.
Proverbs 11:5 (MSG)

You have heard it before, but it deserves repeating—"your character matters." Everything about Christianity begins internally rather than externally. God has always professed to look past the outward appearances of man and look inward at his heart (1 Sam. 16:7). Worship is a matter of the heart. Giving is a matter of the heart. Praise is a matter of the heart. Salvation is a matter of the heart. And happiness is a matter of the heart (not circumstances).

> Proverbs 4:23—*Keep thy heart with all diligence; for out of it are the issues of life.*

It should not be a great surprise to you that happiness is directly proportional to the character of your heart. If your happiness meter is not what you desire it to be, check your character.

One of the greatest passages of the Bible to read on Christian character is found in Matthew 5. In this chapter Jesus taught a series of teachings collectively known as the Sermon on the Mount. These teachings center on true righteousness and godly character.

The Pharisees had deceived themselves into believing that

the righteousness and happiness of a person was found in their outward deeds. Jesus, however, sets the record straight in His Sermon on the Mount. True happiness is found in possessing sincere heartfelt character. The character found only in having a relationship with God through faith in Jesus Christ.

The Beatitudes, Jesus' decrees on blessedness, offer a striking and descriptive image of a true disciple of God. Representing the kingdom of God, they share the suggested character of each citizen. Happiness is clearly the God-desired state of the kingdom and its citizens. Therefore, as a citizen of the kingdom of God, you have the God-ordained right to be happy. You just have to follow the decrees of the King.

> Matthew 5:3–9 (AMP)—*Blessed (happy, to be envied, and spiritually prosperous—with life-joy and satisfaction in God's favor and salvation, regardless of their outward conditions) are the poor in spirit (the humble, who rate themselves insignificant), for theirs is the kingdom of heaven!*
>
> *Blessed and enviably happy [with a happiness produced by the experience of God's favor and especially conditioned by the revelation of His matchless grace] are those who mourn, for they shall be comforted!*
>
> *Blessed (happy, blithesome, joyous, spiritually prosperous—with life-joy and satisfaction in God's favor and salvation, regardless of their outward conditions) are the meek (the mild, patient, long-suffering), for they shall inherit the earth!*
>
> *Blessed and fortunate and happy and spiritually prosperous (in that state in which the born-again child of God enjoys His favor and salvation) are those who hunger and thirst for righteousness (uprightness and right standing with God), for they shall be completely satisfied!*

Blessed (happy, to be envied, and spiritually prosperous—with life-joy and satisfaction in God's favor and salvation, regardless of their outward conditions) are the merciful, for they shall obtain mercy!

Blessed (happy, enviably fortunate, and spiritually prosperous—possessing the happiness produced by the experience of God's favor and especially conditioned by the revelation of His grace, regardless of their outward conditions) are the pure in heart, for they shall see God!

Blessed (enjoying enviable happiness, spiritually prosperous—with life-joy and satisfaction in God's favor and salvation, regardless of their outward conditions) are the makers and maintainers of peace, for they shall be called the sons of God!

Seven kingdom characteristics are found in these first seven verses of the Sermon on the Mount (v.3–9). Each of these characteristics comes with the promise of happiness and blessedness. Therefore it is imperative to your happiness that you have a change of attitude—and walk as a kingdom citizen rather than an outsider.

Poor in spirit

The "poor in spirit" are those who have a full dependence on God, not on themselves. To be poor in spirit means to be correct in your judgment of yourself; it is a person who understands that they are powerless without the help of God Almighty.

Romans 12:3 (AMP)—For by the grace (unmerited favor of God) given to me I warn everyone among you not to estimate and think of himself more highly than he ought [not to have an exaggerated opinion of his own importance], but to rate his ability with sober judgment, each according to the degree of faith apportioned by God to him.

John 5:19–30—*Then answered Jesus and said unto them, Verily, verily, I say unto you, The Son can do nothing of himself, but what he seeth the Father do: for what things soever he doeth, these also doeth the Son likewise. For as the Father hath life in himself; so hath he given to the Son to have life in himself; And hath given him authority to execute judgment also, because he is the Son of man. I can of mine own self do nothing: as I hear, I judge: and my judgment is just; because I seek not mine own will, but the will of the Father which hath sent me.*

Jesus is one of the greatest examples to follow when it comes to being poor in spirit. In John 5:19, 26, 27, and 30, Jesus exemplified a life that is destitute without the love of God in it. Our Savior expressed His direct dependence upon God the Father. He, in essence, declared, *in Him I live, and move, and have my being.* Jesus stated three things given to Him by the Father: aim, ability, and authority. His attitude toward these gifts is clear: it is of God (*I can do nothing*), and it is for God (*I seek not my own will*).

Simply stated, to be poor in spirit means you are able to receive the very divine and supernatural gifts of God and remain levelheaded and focused, knowing that it is of God's strength and for God's pleasure.

Zechariah 4:6—*Then he answered and spake unto me, saying, This is the word of the LORD unto Zerubbabel, saying, Not by might, nor by power, but by my spirit, saith the LORD of hosts.*

Revelation 4:11—*Thou art worthy, O Lord, to receive glory and honour and power: for thou hast created all things, and for thy pleasure they are and were created.*

God's pleasure is seen when we dedicate our lives to His

service and will. Jesus declared, in Mark 12:29–31, that the greatest two things we can ever do is: "Love your God with all your heart, and with all your soul, and with all your mind, and with all your strength…and love your neighbor as yourself." So when He bestows upon us the riches of the kingdom, we remain loyal to His pleasure and do not become sidetracked with our own selfish agendas.

Mourn

To be "poor in spirit" is a mental understanding of one's need. To "mourn" is an emotional response when one discovers he is "poor in spirit." Emotionally one bows down in heaviness and grief. Finally the reality of the situation sets in: *There is nothing I can do! It is in God's hands.* It is like the immense bereavement and crying that occurs over the death of a loved one. It is grief—grief over sin, personal and public, and grief over the fact that our sins are to blame for the death of Jesus Christ. Such mourning will encourage you to walk in holiness, which, in turn, will produce happiness in your life.

> James 4:9 (AMP)—*[As you draw near to God] be deeply penitent and grieve, even weep [over your disloyalty]. Let your laughter be turned to grief and your mirth to dejection and heartfelt shame [for your sins].*

One example of such mourning is Samson during his final days (Judg. 16:23–30). Samson had lost his strength, his dignity, and his sight. The Philistines were preparing to have a great celebration unto their god, and the leaders called Samson to come into the arena so that they could ridicule him. As Samson approached the arena, he asked the person leading him to stop at the pillars that supported the arena. Then Samson cried out unto the Lord: *There is nothing I can do! It is in your hands! God, please help me!* This cry was a cry for forgiveness, a cry for mercy, and a cry of acknowledgment.

> Judges 16:28 (NIV)—*Then Samson prayed to the LORD, "O Sovereign LORD, remember me. O God, please strengthen me just once more, and let me with one blow get revenge on the Philistines for my two eyes.*

When was the last time you cried out to God in response to a mental revelation "There is nothing I can do! It is in God's hands"?

Meek

To be "meek" means to be willing to totally submit to the will of God. It does not mean to be weak or without a backbone. The Greek word for meek denotes "power under control." Meekness involves the will. It is not a spiritual or mental understanding ("poor in spirit") or an emotional response ("mourning"); it is a decided choice. Will I humble myself under the mighty hand of God? Will I submit to His will, way, and word? There are many choices in life, but the meek person will always submit their will to God's will. Will you? Both Moses and Jesus were meek men.

> Numbers 12:3 (AMP)—*Now the man Moses was very meek (gentle, kind, and humble) or above all the men on the face of the earth.*

> Matthew 11:29 (AMP)—*Take My yoke upon you and learn of Me, for I am gentle (meek) and humble (lowly) in heart, and you will find rest (relief and ease and refreshment and recreation and blessed quiet) for your souls.*

James encouraged his audience to develop the character of meekness, stating that it will eventually bring honor to their lives.

> James 4:10 (AMP)—*Humble yourselves [feeling very insignificant] in the presence of the Lord, and He will exalt you [He will lift you up and make your lives significant].*

Hunger and thirst after righteousness

The words "hunger" and "thirst" denote a spiritual appetite longing to be satisfied. To possess this characteristic means one is continually striving to get in right-standing with God. It has become a passion and obsession to draw closer to the Almighty.

> Psalms 42:1–2 (AMP)—*The Psalmist paints a wonderful picture of this characteristic: THE hart pants and longs for the water brooks, so I pant and long for You, O God. My inner self thirsts for God, for the living God. When shall I come and behold the face of God?*

This particular characteristic helps to explain the urgency of this book. The world is "longing for happiness" and becoming more and more frustrated each day. It is my greatest objective, however, to empower you to cease your longing for happiness and launch a new pursuit. The pursuit of righteousness is the pathway to biblical happiness.

Look at how the world contradicts this fact. Happy is he who hungers and thirsts after happiness…not true! Righteousness is the way to happiness. A minister whom I respect describes righteousness as "clean living." I am blessed, happy, fortunate, well off, in position, and to be envied because I live a clean life.

The Psalmist in Psalm 112 shared blessings that are connected to living a clean life—walking in righteousness—legacy, prosperity, direction, character, integrity, discretion, and stability.

> Psalms 112:1–7—*Praise ye the LORD. Blessed is the man that feareth the LORD, that delighteth greatly in his commandments. His seed shall be mighty upon earth: the generation of the upright shall be blessed. Wealth and riches shall be in his house: and his righteousness endureth for ever. Unto the upright there ariseth light in the darkness: he is gracious, and full of compassion, and*

righteous. A good man sheweth favour, and lendeth: he will guide his affairs with discretion. Surely he shall not be moved for ever: the righteous shall be in everlasting remembrance. He shall not be afraid of evil tidings: his heart is fixed, trusting in the LORD.

Merciful

Just as God has shown mercy to you, this characteristic requires you to show mercy (compassion) to others. Jesus declared in Luke 6:36, "Be ye therefore merciful, as your Father also is merciful." Mercy denotes compassion, pity, kindness, forgiveness, and benevolence. As I mentioned in an earlier chapter, God has set two ongoing commandments before us: walk before Him in holiness (this is true love to God) and have unrelenting mercy upon your neighbor.

Matthew 18:21–22 (NIV)—*Then Peter came to Jesus and asked, "Lord, how many times shall I forgive my brother when he sins against me? Up to seven times?" Jesus answered, "I tell you, not seven times, but seventy-seven times.*

When Peter asked Jesus about forgiveness, in Matthew 18:21–35, he set a limit or cutoff to the number of times he was to show mercy. But Jesus, in His infinite wisdom, declared unto Peter that mercy should never be limited. Peter said 7 times, and Jesus said 490 times—meaning it should be ongoing. Afterward, Jesus spoke a parable concerning an unmerciful servant. The servant owed a great amount of money to his lord, so he pleaded for forgiveness of the debt. The lord gained him favor. The servant, however—after being forgiven of debt—went out, found a fellow servant who owed him money, and demanded payment. When the lord discovered the incident, he summoned the servant before him and tormented him because the servant failed to reciprocate the mercy he had received.

> Matthew 18:32–35—*Then his lord, after that he had called him, said unto him, O thou wicked servant, I forgave thee all that debt, because thou desiredst me: Shouldest not thou also have had compassion on thy fellowservant, even as I had pity on thee? And his lord was wroth, and delivered him to the tormentors, till he should pay all that was due unto him. So likewise shall my heavenly Father do also unto you, if ye from your hearts forgive not every one his brother their trespasses.*

The same warning is for you and me. We must show mercy to others because our Lord has shown mercy to us. Are you showing mercy?

Pure in heart

Sincere, earnest, single, and unselfish are words that describe what our motives should be. When we speak, do, act, go, help, or be silent, our motives should exemplify godly character. This particular characteristic goes totally contrary to the thought processes of modern society. Today the motives behind many actions are greed, selfishness, hatred, lust, and malice. And it is because of this misdirection of motives many people are not finding happiness and are resorting to violence. You read about tragic stories of murder, harassment, assault, and rape everyday. And each story has something in common: they are fueled by the misdirection of motives.

> James 4:1–3—*From whence come wars and fightings among you? come they not hence, even of your lusts that war in your members? Ye lust, and have not: ye kill, and desire to have, and cannot obtain: ye fight and war, yet ye have not, because ye ask not. Ye ask, and receive not, because ye ask amiss, that ye may consume it upon your lusts.*

In the Sermon on the Mount, one important statement Jesus

made was, "For I say unto you, That except your righteousness shall exceed the righteousness of the scribes and Pharisees, ye shall in no case enter into the kingdom of heaven" (Matt. 5:20).

Exceeding the righteousness of the Pharisees and scribes involved changing one's motives in life; Jesus spent a good duration of time teaching this lesson. In Matthew 6 He spent time discussing the right motives toward giving, praying, fasting, and material things. The Bible declares that the "pure in heart" are blessed.

> Colossians 3:17—*And whatsoever ye do in word or deed, do all in the name of the Lord Jesus, giving thanks to God and the Father by him.*

> Colossians 3:23—*And whatsoever ye do, do it heartily, as to the Lord, and not unto men.*

Peacemaker

Christians should be characterized as peacemakers. Peacemakers are people who bring others together. The biblical role of peacemaker is threefold.

First the peacemaker is a person who strives to make peace with God. He conquers the inner struggle, settles the inner tension, and handles the inner pressure. He takes the struggle within his heart between good and evil and strives for the good and conquers the bad. Paul demonstrated this type of peacemaker in Romans 5:1: "Therefore being justified by faith, we have peace with God through our Lord Jesus Christ." He continued this thought in Ephesians 2:14: "For he is our peace, who hath made both one, and hath broken down the middle wall of partition between us."

Second the peacemaker is a person who strives at every opportunity to make peace within others. He seeks and leads others to make their peace with God—to conquer their inner struggle, to settle their inner tension, to handle their inner pressure. Paul wrote about this type of peacemaker in 2 Corinthians 5:18: "And all things are of God, who hath reconciled us to himself by Jesus Christ, and hath given to us the ministry of reconciliation."

Third the peacemaker is a person who strives at every opportunity to make peace between others. He works to solve disputes and erase divisions, to reconcile differences and eliminate strife, to silence tongues and build relationships. Paul referred to this role of peacemaker in 2 Corinthians 13:11: "Finally, brethren, farewell. Be perfect, be of good comfort, be of one mind, live in peace; and the God of love and peace shall be with you." The writer of Hebrews referred to it in Hebrews 12:14: "Follow peace with all men, and holiness, without which no man shall see the Lord." Peter referred to it in 1 Peter 3:11: "Let him eschew evil, and do good; let him seek peace, and ensue it." Even James referred to it in James 3:18: "and the fruit of righteousness is sown in peace of them that make peace."

Questions to Ask and Answer

1. What comes to mind, or how does it make you feel, when you discover that some of Jesus' first words to his disciples and the multitude were words of happy living?

2. Dr. Turner mentioned in the first paragraph of this chapter that happiness, like worship, praise, and giving, is a matter of the heart. Spend some time reflecting on this thought. (Read Psalm 57:7.)

3. Which characteristic(s) describes you? Which characteristic(s) do you find most challenging?

4. How do you plan to overcome the barriers and achieve your God-ordained happiness?

Chapter 7

Your Character is Important

Memory Verse: Proverbs 11:5 (MSG)—*Moral character makes for smooth traveling; an evil life is a hard life.*

1. Dr. Turner said, "Happiness is a matter of the heart (not circumstances)." Take a moment to reflect on the statement and write your thoughts.

_____

_____

_____

_____

_____

2. Because your Christian character is so critical to being Christlike and happy, let's dig deeper into each feature of the characteristics of the Beatitudes. Define each of the seven features, and indicate two ways you can help manifest each in your life more fully.

Poor in Spirit means _____

_____

    I can help manifest this by_____

_____

Mourn means _____

_____

    I can help manifest this by_____

_____

Meek means _____

_____

    I can help manifest this by_____

_____

Hunger and Thirst after righteousness means _____

_____

    I can help manifest this by_____

_____

Merciful means _____

_____

    I can help manifest this by_____

_____

Pure in Heart means _____

_____

    I can help manifest this by_____

_____

Peacemaker means _____

_____

    I can help manifest this by_____

_____

3. Dr. Turner said, "True happiness is found in possessing sincere heartfelt character." Reflect on this statement. Read Proverb 11:5 aloud. What are your thoughts?

_____

_____

_____

_____

Chapter 8

The Happy Experience

The thief does not come except to steal, and to kill, and to destroy. I have come that they may have life, and that they may have it more abundantly.
John 10:10 (NKJV)

Esher and makarios are defined as experiencing a state of happiness and blessedness. But what does the Bible have to say about this "happy experience." What should you, a devoted Christian walking in the state of happiness, expect?

Victory over your enemies

> Deuteronomy 33:29 (AMP)—*Happy are you, O Israel, and blessing is yours! Who is like you, a people saved by the Lord, the Shield of your help, the Sword that exalts you! Your enemies shall come fawning and cringing, and submit feigned obedience to you, and you shall march on their high places.*

God intervened and released His Son, Jesus, from glory, so you and I might have a right to the tree of life. God has made salvation available to every man and woman on the face of the earth. His only requirement is that we accept salvation on His terms—through His Son, Jesus. If you have accepted Jesus as your Savior, you are saved. "Happy are you...Who is like you, a people saved by the Lord" (Deut. 33:29).

It is apparent, from this verse, the salvation of God's chosen people included an element of victory. Based upon their identity with the Father, God swore to become their shield—their help, strength, and defense. Such is the case with all who are saved. God gives us victory over our enemies!

> Proverbs 16:7—*When a man's ways please the LORD, he maketh even his enemies to be at peace with him.*

David, on several occasions, testified of God's ability to lift him above his enemies. David could experience victory because he was saved by God and he was walking in the will of God (i.e., trusting, fearing, doing, and being).

> Psalms 27:1–2—*The LORD is my light and my salvation; whom shall I fear? the LORD is the strength of my life; of whom shall I be afraid? When the wicked, even mine enemies and my foes, came upon me to eat up my flesh, they stumbled and fell.*

Prosperous living

It has been a difficult thing to convince believers that there are an abundance of Bible verses that promote a Christian's prosperity. Prosperity within the Body of Christ has become taboo. If you are prosperous or talk about prosperity, then you have left the straight and narrow path. Not true!

The Bible spends a great deal of time talking about the prosperity of the righteous and upright. The apostle John wrote Gaius wishing him prosperity in, above all things, his body and soul (3 John 1–2). God promised Joshua prosperity and success in his leadership of the children of Israel (Josh. 1:8). Daniel prospered as he served the true and living God under two kings (Dan. 6:28). As Elihu made his appeal to Job to fear the Lord, he stated that when a person repents and returns to God—they spend their days in prosperity and years in pleasure (Job 36:11).

The Happy Experience

Happiness has always been accompanied with prosperous living.

Psalm 1:3—*And he shall be like a tree planted by the rivers of water, that bringeth forth his fruit in his season; his leaf also shall not wither; and whatsoever he doeth shall prosper.*

Psalm 112:2-3 (AMP)—*His [spiritual] offspring shall be mighty upon earth; the generation of the upright shall be blessed. Prosperity and welfare are in his house, and his righteousness endures forever.*

Proverbs 3:16-18 (NKJV)—*Length of days is in her right hand, In her left hand riches and honor. Her ways are ways of pleasantness, And all her paths are peace. She is a tree of life to those who take hold of her, And happy are all who retain her.*

The Psalmist, in Psalm 1:1-2, concluded that happiness is found in being mindful of one's surrounding, environment, and company and by continually mediating on the Word of God. In verse 3 he showed the happy experience that follows happiness. The experience is vibrant, fruitful, enduring, and prosperous.

The Psalmist, in Psalm 112:1 stated that happiness is found in the fear of the Lord and the keeping of His commandments. In verse 2 he gave the happy experience that follows happiness. The experience in this psalm conveys prosperity that is generational and personal.

King Solomon, in Proverbs 3:13, talked about the extreme happiness that follows a person who is willing to find wisdom and get understanding. In verses 16-18 he described the various blessings that develop from walking and living in wisdom and understanding. These blessings involve longevity, prosperity, honor, appeal, peace, and vitality.

God's Glory upon You

It has been well established that the happy state does not exempt us from persecution. Any Christian truly living for God, walking in His will, and enjoying the abundant life that only God can give—will be persecuted. David declared it best when he wrote of the severe persecution the righteous will encounter in life.

> Psalms 34:19 (BBE)—*Great are the troubles of the upright: but the Lord takes him safely out of them all.*

> 1 Peter 4:14 (AMP)—*If you are censured and suffer abuse [because you bear] the name of Christ, blessed [are you—happy, fortunate, to be envied, with life-joy, and satisfaction in God's favor and salvation, regardless of your outward condition], because the Spirit of glory, the Spirit of God, is resting upon you. On their part He is blasphemed, but on your part He is glorified.*

The apostle Peter wrote of the happiness that comes even in persecution. You can be happy even when your enemies are attempting to cause you brutal pain. David said God would prepare a table before us in the presence of our enemies (Ps. 23:5). You can be happy because you are following in the steps of Jesus Christ, fellowshipping in His suffering.

As he wrote about the happiness that comes in persecution, Peter also wrote about the experience that takes place. In persecution God's glory rests upon the believer. There is no other time that a Christian feels more at oneness with God than in persecution. This is why happiness is so overwhelming, because you will sense the presence of God in your life. Imagine that, life in and of itself could be terrible—but in the spiritual realm you are better off than before. Your testimony is stronger. You are bringing more glory to God than ever before.

> 2 Corinthians 12:9–10 (NKJV)—*And He said to me, "My grace is sufficient for you, for My strength is made perfect in weakness." Therefore most gladly I will rather boast in my infirmities, that the power of Christ may rest upon me. Therefore I take pleasure in infirmities, in reproaches, in needs, in persecutions, in distresses, for Christ's sake. For when I am weak, then I am strong.*

The apostle Paul himself discovered this vital lesson when he received a thorn in his flesh. He prayed three times for God to remove the thorn, but God refused and instead offered Paul something greater: His grace. Upon understanding God's grace and intent, Paul's perception changed. He fully understood that the glory of God rested upon him, and he was in the presence of God more than ever before. Happiness filled his body, so much that he declared the pleasure he would take in the infirmities, reproaches, needs, persecutions, and distresses, for Christ's sake. Paul concluded his thought by stating that he is stronger with God in the worst circumstance than without God in the best situation.

Fearlessness

Throughout Scripture it has been repeated: Do not be afraid! God told Moses. God told Joshua. He told Jeremiah. He told the children of Israel. He told a host of believers. In the New Testament, Jesus on a regular basis told His disciples. Paul wrote these words concerning Christians in 2 Timothy 1:7: "For God has not given us a spirit of fear."

Based upon the overwhelming evidence, it is clear that the will of God for Christians is fearlessness. Our lives should not be lived in fear, doubt, uncertainty and worry but in peace, joy, and happiness. We are standing on a sure foundation.

> Hebrews 13:6 (MSG)—*We can boldly quote, God is there, ready to help; I'm fearless no matter what. Who or*

what can get to me?

1 Peter 3:14–16 (BBE)—But you are happy if you undergo pain because of righteousness; have no part in their fear and do not be troubled; But give honour to Christ in your hearts as your Lord; and be ready at any time when you are questioned about the hope which is in you, to give an answer in the fear of the Lord and without pride; Being conscious that you have done no wrong; so that those who say evil things about your good way of life as Christians may be put to shame.

Peter emphasized this point in 1 Peter 3:14–16. This passage centers on the certain suffering Christians will endure as they live lives that are conformed to the image of Christ. First he wrote happiness is found in suffering for the sake of righteousness. Then he further explained what the happy experience will afford the Christian. Peter declared be fearless, do not worry, give honor and praise to God, speak up concerning your faith, walk in blamelessness, and await your enemy's demise.

A Crown of Life (Eternal Life)

James 1:12 (AMP)—Blessed (happy, to be envied) is the man who is patient under trial and stands up under temptation, for when he has stood the test and been approved, he will receive [the victor's] crown of life which God has promised to those who love Him.

In James 1:12 James talked about the happiness that comes from enduring temptation as a good soldier. He also talked about the happy experience that is found in the life of one who has endured temptation. To that person James declared that the crown of life will be awarded. The phrase "crown of life" denotes life itself. The person who lives and endures temptation until the end will receive something far more valuable than any earthly jewel: life with no end.

Revelation 2:10—*Fear none of those things which thou shalt suffer: behold, the devil shall cast some of you into prison, that ye may be tried; and ye shall have tribulation ten days: be thou faithful unto death, and I will give thee a crown of life.*

Favor and Joy

I grew up hearing Christians declare how they did not want happiness, but they wanted joy. They exclaimed that happiness was of the world and joy was of God. I kindly disagree. I believe happiness and joy, if biblical, are of God. I believe God wants us to be happy and have joy. Furthermore, I believe joy is an important element of the happy state in which God desires believers to live.

Psalms 89:15–17 (BBE)—*Happy are the people who have knowledge of the holy cry: the light of your face, O Lord, will be shining on their way. In your name will they have joy all the day: in your righteousness will they be lifted up.*

After expounding on the Lord's mighty character and power, the Psalmist, in Psalm 89:15–17 (AMP), exhorted the people to praise God in the highest. He accomplished this task by telling them their praise would be a pathway to happiness: "Blessed (happy, fortunate, to be envied) are the people who know the joyful sound." Praise has always had a way of lifting downtrodden souls and broken spirits.

The Psalmist gave a wonderful picture of what the promised happiness resembled. Simply put, it is a life of God's favor and unspeakable joy. The light of God's face will continually shine in the direction of those who are happy. Plus, at the very thought or mention of His name, joy will fill the atmosphere. This is such an uplifting passage of Scripture. My happiness opens the door to God's very presence.

Proverbs 8:32–36 (BBE)—Give ear to me then, my sons: for happy are those who keep my ways. Take my teaching and be wise; do not let it go. Happy is the man who gives ear to me, watching at my doors day by day, keeping his place by the pillars of my house. For whoever gets me gets life, and grace from the Lord will come to him. But he who does evil to me, does wrong to his soul: all my haters are in love with death.

In Proverbs 8:32–36, Solomon wrote that happiness comes in response to attaining wisdom and walking in obedience. As it pertains to the happy experience, he shared the same belief as the Psalmist. Once happiness is achieved, it opens the door to joy and favor. In verse 35 he wrote that the happy person gets life (meaning, destiny, purpose, and joy) and grace (unmerited favor) from the Lord.

Questions to Ask and Answer

1. Have you accepted the happiness that only God can provide?

2. What are your personal expectations of this happiness? As a devoted Christian, what six expectations of happiness does the Bible give?

3. How important is it to continually expect and profess what has been promised—even in the midst of trials and tribulations? (Read Proverbs 23:7; 18:21.)

4. Do you find it hard to look for these proven expectations for believers? Why?

5. Whose report will you believe…God's or man's? (Read Psalms 18:30; 118:8.)

Chapter 8

The Happy Experience

Memory Verse: John 10:10–11 (AMP)—*The thief comes only in order to steal and kill and destroy. I came that they may have and enjoy life, and have it in abundance (to the full, till it overflows). 11 I am the Good Shepherd. The Good Shepherd risks and lays down His [own] life for the sheep.*

1. Dr. Turner said, "The words 'esher' and 'makarios' are defined as experiencing a state of happiness and blessedness." Explain your concept of a state of happiness and blessedness.

_____

_____

_____

_____

_____

_____

2. How would you describe the correlation between victory over your enemies and being happy?

_____

_____

_____

_____

3. Proverb 16:7 says, "When a man's ways please the LORD, he maketh even his enemies to be at peace with him." Reflect and describe your thoughts on the correlation between your happiness and God's satisfaction.

_____

_____

_____

_____

When God is satisfied, you will be happy. Reflect on the various ways your happiness is experienced and list them.

_____

_____

_____

_____

_____

4. In great detail describe your personal belief on the prosperity of the upright. Is it God-ordained or man-made?

_____

_____

_____

_____

_____

_____

5. Dr. Turner concluded, "Furthermore, I believe that joy is an important element of the happy state in which God desires believers to live." Read Psalm 89:15–17 aloud. Reflect and write your thoughts.

_____

_____

_____

_____

6. Read 1 Peter 3:14–16 aloud. Describe the happiness of Christians who suffer for righteousness.

_____

_____

_____

_____

7. Reflect and write your thoughts on your commitment to living the happy experience. Please include specific and immediate plans for implementation into your daily life.

Appendix

Faith Confessions of Happiness

So let us seize and hold fast and retain without wavering the hope we cherish and confess and our acknowledgement of it, for He Who promised is reliable (sure) and faithful to His word.
Hebrews 10:23 (AMP)

- I am blessed! I am supremely happy! God has a divine plan for my happiness.

- I am blessed! I am supremely happy! The Bible is the unadulterated Word of God, and it proclaims happiness for Christians.

- I am blessed! I am supremely happy! I accept my happiness though faith.

- I am blessed! I am supremely happy! I am saved.

- I am blessed! I am supremely happy! My happiness is not linked to the world's happiness.

- I am blessed! I am supremely happy! My happiness is not contingent on my external state or circumstance.

- I am blessed! I am supremely happy! Whether or not the world understands or validates it.

- I am blessed! I am supremely happy! I currently cannot perceive it with my five common senses, but I trust God and His Word.

- I am blessed! I am supremely happy! I am a child of God.

- I am blessed! I am supremely happy! My happiness is solely rooted in my relationship with God.

- I am blessed! I am supremely happy! My happiness is a gift of God.

- I am blessed! I am supremely happy! My happiness will lead to limitless success.

- I am blessed! I am supremely happy! I am fortunate, spiritually prosperous, to be envied, joyous, and blithesome.

- I am blessed! I am supremely happy! I remain happy despite storms, disappointments, shortfalls, and tribulations.

- I am blessed! I am supremely happy! God wants me to be happy.

- I am blessed! I am supremely happy! God knows the plans He has for me, plans to prosper me and not to harm me, plans to give me hope and a future.

- I am blessed! I am supremely happy! God has graciously and mercifully worked on my behalf.

- I am blessed! I am supremely happy! God has chosen and called me.

- I am blessed! I am supremely happy! I have been forgiven, covered, and relieved.

- I am blessed! I am supremely happy! God cares enough to discipline me and lead me in the paths of righteousness.

- I am blessed! I am supremely happy! I fear God.

Faith Confessions of Happiness

- I am blessed! I am supremely happy! I have made Jesus my Lord.

- I am blessed! I am supremely happy! I am solely depending on God.

- I am blessed! I am supremely happy! I am walking in the wisdom and understanding of God Almighty.

- I am blessed! I am supremely happy! I believe that God deserves the highest worship.

- I am blessed! I am supremely happy! I am not offended by the Word of God.

- I am blessed! I am supremely happy! I have endured temptation.

- I am blessed! I am supremely happy! God is a God of a second chance.

- I am blessed! I am supremely happy! There is no condemnation to those in Christ Jesus who do not walk after the flesh but after the Spirit.

- I am blessed! I am supremely happy! I have dedicated and am dedicating my life to positioning myself for happiness.

- I am blessed! I am supremely happy! I am a doer of the Word.

- I am blessed! I am supremely happy! I am walking in holiness.

- I am blessed! I am supremely happy! I am walking in justice; I am treating my neighbor fairly.

- I am blessed! I am supremely happy! I wait patiently on the Lord for deliverance.

- I am blessed! I am supremely happy! I willingly suffer for Christ's sake, for righteousness.

- I am blessed! I am supremely happy! I am confident of my Christian walk.

- I am blessed! I am supremely happy! God supplies all of my needs.

- I am blessed! I am supremely happy! I see sin as God sees sin: I hate it.

- I am blessed! I am supremely happy! I understand that wisdom is found in a multitude of counselors.

- I am blessed! I am supremely happy! I constantly hunger and thirst for righteousness, and God satisfies me.

- I am blessed! I am supremely happy! I forgive others as God has forgiven me.

- I am blessed! I am supremely happy! I enjoy clean living.

- I am blessed! I am supremely happy! I am a minister of reconciliation.

- I am blessed! I am supremely happy! I serve as a peacemaker not a troublemaker.

- I am blessed! I am supremely happy! I have victory over my enemies.

- I am blessed! I am supremely happy! I am more than a conqueror.

- I am blessed! I am supremely happy! I will overcome.

Faith Confessions of Happiness

- I am blessed! I am supremely happy! I am prosperous.

- I am blessed! I am supremely happy! I have goodly success.

- I am blessed! I am supremely happy! I have divine overflow.

- I am blessed! I am supremely happy! God's glory rests on my life.

- I am blessed! I am supremely happy! I do not have a spirit of fear, but of love, power, and a sound mind.

- I am blessed! I am supremely happy! I have eternal life; I will live forever.

- I am blessed! I am supremely happy! I have the countenance of God's face shining in my direction.

- I am blessed! I am supremely happy! I have God's favor.

- I am blessed! I am supremely happy! I have Jesus' joy.

- I am blessed! I am supremely happy! The world does not give me joy and the world cannot take my joy.

- I am blessed! I am supremely happy! The kingdom of heaven belongs to me.

- I am blessed! I am supremely happy! I am a citizen of God's kingdom.

- I am blessed! I am supremely happy! I am in this world but not of this world.

- I am blessed! I am supremely happy! God has comforted me.

- I am blessed! I am supremely happy! My children are blessed.

- I am blessed! I am supremely happy! I have inherited the earth, presently and eternally.

- I am blessed! I am supremely happy! My children will be blessed.

- I am blessed! I am supremely happy! My children's children will be blessed.

- I am blessed! I am supremely happy! My life is in God's hands.

- I am blessed! I am supremely happy! God is an awesome God.

- I am blessed! I am supremely happy! God is my healer.

- I am blessed! I am supremely happy! God is my battle-axe.

- I am blessed! I am supremely happy! God is my friend.

- I am blessed! I am supremely happy! God is my hope for tomorrow.

- I am blessed! I am supremely happy! God is my loin tamer.

- I am blessed! I am supremely happy! God is my bridge over troubled waters.

- I am blessed! I am supremely happy! God is my guide.

- I am blessed! I am supremely happy! I'm free.

- I am blessed! I am supremely happy! I have purpose.

- I am blessed! I am supremely happy! I am no longer bound; no more chains are holding me.

About the Author

Marcus E. Turner, Sr. has been the senior pastor of Beulah Baptist Church since 1999. He serves as the principal overseer, primary shepherd, and prophetic visionary of the congregation. Dr. Turner has written countless manuscripts on theological matters, conducted lectures for several professional organizations, and broadcasted in more than eight states.

As the nucleus for community development in Deanwood Heights, Dr. Turner has served as the chairman and president of Beulah Community Improvement Corporation since 2001. In his role of president, he has formulated and presented revolutionary policies and planning recommendations to the board of directors. Dr. Turner is currently guiding two affordable housing development projects: Eden Place at Beulah Crossing, a sixty-three-unit townhome development, and Eastbrooke at Beulah Crossing, a thirty-nine-unit rental apartment development. In addition he has written proposals and secured public and private funding for community programming, which has brought a multiplicity of human services to the community, such as, GED, adult education, affordable housing, health promotion, clothes drive, food, outreach, youth & senior programming, computer training, and economic development.

Dr. Turner has developed curriculum for various institutions and has taught on different levels, including the post-secondary level. Currently he serves as a faculty member with the University of Phoenix. He received his Doctor of Ministry (D.Min) in 1999 and Master of Business Administration (MBA) in 2009.

He has been married for seventeen years and is the father of four children.

For a live presentation of the material found in *Realizing Happiness: A Perceptive Study of Biblical Happiness* or other information on Dr. Turner's availability and ministry contact:

information@realizingyourhappiness.com
or
www.realizingyourhappiness.com/publisher.html

Realizing Happiness: A Perceptive Study of Biblical Happiness is available at **www.realizingyourhappiness.com**, www.beulahministries.org, any online bookstore (e.g. www.amazon.com), or your local Christian bookstore.

For the best priced bulk book orders of *Realizing Happiness: A Perceptive Study of Biblical Happiness* contact:

information@realizingyourhappiness.com
or
www.realizingyourhappiness.com/tour.html

www.ingramcontent.com/pod-product-compliance
Lightning Source LLC
Chambersburg PA
CBHW070503100426
42743CB00010B/1738